CIVILITY
Unleashed

Using
Civility
to Survive
and Thrive in
the Workplace

DIANA DAMRON

PO Box 2675
Kalispell, MT 59903
(406) 890-8453
Diana@DianaDamron.com
www.DianaDamron.com

Graphic design by Brenda Hawkes

Edited by Phyllis Jask

Author photos by B. Victoria Wojciechowski

Printed in the United States of America

ISBN-13: 978-1530312429

ISBN-10: 1530312426

PRAISE FOR *CIVILITY UNLEASHED*

Every day, customers define your company by the civility of its employees! Ask yourself, what do customers see in your employees? Do customers line up to do business or run for the exits? Diana Damron's solutions represent a fresh way of thinking. Follow her custom, self-guiding path to a more profitable, efficient, and effective civil work environment!

—Stephen P. Behringer, Procter & Gamble Senior Sales Technology Manager, Kmart Senior Vice President

Caught up in a toxic work environment? It can affect your life and attitude both on and off the job. Diana Damron has penned this book to help you diagnose your situation, evaluate your position, and assess your next steps. She sets forth a helpful approach to analyzing the causes of workplace incivility, and provides intuitive and introspective analysis of possible causes and steps to be taken to correct the condition, and perhaps most importantly, to protect yourself.

—David A. Ogden, Attorney at Law, and inspiration for the book *The Lincoln Lawyer*

Diana Damron has brilliantly identified the cost of bad behavior and rudeness in America. As a subject-matter expert and professional speaker, Diana knows that the cornerstones of Civility, Communication, and Character are the root of greater success, career opportunity, and personal happiness. I have enjoyed reading every page of this book and plan to gift numerous copies. I particularly liked the wrap-ups at the end of each chapter and Diana's "C's the Day" tips and tools. Each one guides us on how to keep our cool, keep our health and keep relevant in today's sometimes confusing, breakneck speed, and uncertain global workplace environment. This book is a steady rudder we all can use now and then to navigate the turbulent waters of human behavior and relationship building... both at home and on the job.

—Anne Bruce, International Platform Speaker, Coach, and Bestselling Author of *Discover True North*

CONTENTS

Acknowledgments vii

Introduction ix

PART I: Civility 101

Chapter 1: The Force of Civility 3

Chapter 2: Civility's Influence on Corporate Culture................................. 13

Chapter 3: Incivility: The Dark Side of Bad Behavior................................ 23

Chapter 4: Civility: The Great Equalizer.. 37

PART II: The Civil Business

Chapter 5: Foundation of Civility: Politeness, Respect, and Trust.............. 49

Chapter 6: Obstacles to Civility.. 65

Chapter 7: Elements of Civility... 79

PART III: The Civil Leader

Chapter 8: Establishing and Maintaining Trust.. 93

Chapter 9: Qualities of the Civil Leader... 107

Chapter 10: Why Leaders Must Care... 115

PART IV: The Civil Self

Chapter 11: Exercise Your Civil Self.. 131

Chapter 12: The Civil Self Success Plan... 151

Chapter 13: Protecting Yourself When You're Incivility's Target 163

Conclusion: C's the Day...Day after Day 173

About the Author... 175

Acknowledgments

Writing a book about civility isn't necessarily the best way to test an author's CQ—what I call the Civility Quotient. If you've ever sat down to bring a subject to life and attempted to convince readers to re-think and even discard long-held opinions and behaviors, you know that the writing process can be exasperating at best. For yours truly, there were those delightful times of excitement and inspiration, all too frequently punctuated by periods of frustration and a blank page. Those latter times too often resulted in impatience—not the best fuel for civility.

A book on civility is the culmination of not only research, but real world experience. I have had so many teachers of civility in my life through their example. To all of you, I say a thank you that goes far beyond words.

Thank you, Mother and Dad, for teaching me civility, not only through your daily instruction to express kindness to all, but by your daily examples of what that looks and sounds like. I miss you both every day.

Thank you, Dawn Doyle, for those days and evenings in your classes when you brought civility to life, and later when you mentored me on how to bring civility into the lives of others. Your influence remains with me today. Thank you, John S. Pike, for demonstrating civility in action by keeping your word and pushing me to be better in everything I have chosen to undertake. I will always be grateful for your confidence, your willingness to give me a chance, and your encouragement.

Anne Bruce, you've always been the essence of civility. Your genuine kindness, encouragement, and friendship are treasures for which I will always be grateful. Thank you for being there along this journey as I follow my "True North."

Thank you, Dolly Hinshaw, for those lively conversations about civility and its real impact. They always fueled me to take the next step.

I extend a huge thank you to Stephen Behringer for your incredible patience and support for my adventures in the world of civility. Ever since I embarked, you've been there, whether sitting in on my first workshop or allowing me to constantly barrage you with questions. A special thank you to David Ogden for the hours you spent reading my manuscripts and being my cheerleader. You both gave me the gifts of encouragement and inspiration.

Words alone only scratch the surface of my gratitude toward Catherine Webber for mentoring me through the process of bringing an idea to life. You've been encouraging—yet always honest—along the way. I've leaned on you. You've inspired me and continue to do so.

I thank my marvelous editor, Phyllis Jask. You polished the rough spots and challenged me with your keen insight and did the impossible: you made the entire process so much fun.

Brenda Hawkes, you were able to take my words and ideas and create the perfect cover as well as add eye appeal to the subject of civility. Thank you for your creative magic.

Victoria Wojciechowski, you work magic behind the camera lens not only with your professional expertise but with your personal warmth and joy. I'm grateful for every photo shoot with you.

Finally, thank you to my precious family for your love, support, and ongoing inspiration through the entire process of bringing this book to fruition. I am so grateful for your humor, patience, and genuine civility. I love you with all my heart.

Introduction

It was Christmas Eve. The lights on our tree twinkled through the ornaments that I had placed one by one on its branches. My family moved back and forth between the kitchen and living room quietly, barely making a sound. They'd given up on trying to evoke Yuletide cheer in me, or any cheer for that matter. Outside the snow tumbled softly onto the ground. It was the making of a beautiful holiday, a glorious white Christmas, except for one thing. Me. I was sitting on the couch in tears.

I'd let everyone down, or at least that was what was going through my head. I felt that I'd failed professionally as both a leader and an employee. Throughout my life, I had been the person who could carry on a conversation with a rock and get along with Godzilla, and yet somehow I'd misstepped in a way that set me up to be center stage in ongoing drama in my own workplace. It didn't happen overnight, but eventually, I was out of a job.

I played conversation after conversation over and over in my head to determine what I could have done differently. I repeated to myself that everything that went wrong, professionally, was my fault. (It wasn't.) I reviewed one episode after another to determine how I could have produced a better result. All this replaying, repeating, and reviewing resulted in the same conclusion: I was a failure. I kept telling myself that I should have known better on each and every occasion.

My feelings of loss, ineptitude, and worthlessness didn't vanish each night when I left the building where I worked. Instead, they grabbed hold of my heart and mind. For more than a year, the negativity didn't drop away as I trudged up my steps to walk in my front door. As much as I hoped my feelings of dejection would cling to my coat as I hung it in the closet and leave me in peace, they remained steadfast. Discouragement fastened itself to me, and I failed to find the solvent to dissolve it.

I had become enmeshed in a toxic work environment, and I wasn't alone.

That experience led me to begin investigating what was happening in our workplaces. I thought I was unique, or at least one of the few, caught up in workplace drama. Instead, I learned my experience wasn't uncommon—in fact, it was becoming the norm. What worried me most was that if I felt like an ooey-gooey mess at the end of my tenure, what was happening to other men and women? I was lucky. I came home to a supportive family and had experienced a childhood full of love and encouragement. Yet I still felt miserable. What about those people who didn't have that support of affection and warmth? How must they feel?

As I dived into the research and interviewed people about their current and former work experiences, I learned that in department after department, business after business, agency after agency, toxic environments thrive, while the men and women stuck in them suffer. I recently sat at a table where former employees from different countries but the same industry high-fived one another for surviving and escaping workplaces where leadership tolerated disrespect, undermining, and dishonesty. Each person felt the same. While immersed in that culture, they felt helpless. That evening, however, they felt celebratory!

Now, looking back, I realize my time in toxicity was one of the best experiences of my life! Don't get me wrong—I'm no masochist. However, in hindsight 1 can see the episodes of drama, turmoil, and chaos as opportunities that taught me about influence, power, and emotions. I've learned about my mistakes, my misinterpretations, and some misplaced emotions. The German philosopher Friedrich Nietzsche told us that which does not destroy us makes us stronger. By no means am I equating a toxic work environment to a deadly disease or a battlefield, but toxic work environments can take a dramatic toll on anyone, whether a target of abusive behavior, a participant, or simply an observer of toxic behavior.

Unlike the diagnosis of a fatal illness or the obvious weaponry of a combat zone, a toxic environment doesn't necessarily shock or explode and make itself obvious.

Toxic environments can morph from supportive to destructive. They can be seductive with power and influence, yet hurtful through confusion. The reason for toxic environments can be many; the consequences of toxic environments are never good, positive, or physically, mentally, or emotionally healthy. All toxic environments have one thing in common: they lack civility!

Caught up in the day-to-day, week-to-week, month-to-month drama at work, I wasn't clear about anything. In fact, I mentally took on full responsibility for my situation. No longer could I recognize the truth of a twisted experience for what it truly was. It wasn't until I explained my predicament to a dear friend, who'd spent decades in the business world, that I realized it wasn't all in my head. Her instructions were clear: "Get out!"

Upon my departure, I began to investigate and reflect on my experience. Although I thought mine was a rare episode, I learned quickly that it was far too typical. Our workplaces are rife with fear, anger, confusion, rudeness, incivility, and aggression. As I spoke with people in the private and public sectors, the realms of profit and non-profit, and organizations large and small, I heard a recurring theme: Toxic environments are far from being in short supply. They're rampant. In fact, they are often nurtured through intimidation, confusion, obsessive attitudes of profit over people, and the unwillingness to confront and eradicate.

As I began my study, I found that two women—professors at business schools—had done vast research on the subject of toxic workplaces. In their book *The Cost of Bad Behavior*, Christine Pearson and Christine Porath make the case that turning a blind eye to rude behavior's first blush in the workplace costs employers big bucks.

But my reason for addressing the subject of toxic environments was far more personal. I didn't want anyone to feel what I felt, to go through what I went through, and to affect their loved ones' lives in the way that I had. I wanted employers and employees, bosses and staff, the influencer at the top, and the unaware influencer at the bottom to realize that each of us influences our workplace, and that we affect one another.

My work led me to uncover three critical elements that are essential and vital to our lives—yours and mine. I call them **The 3 C's: Civility, Communication, and Character**.

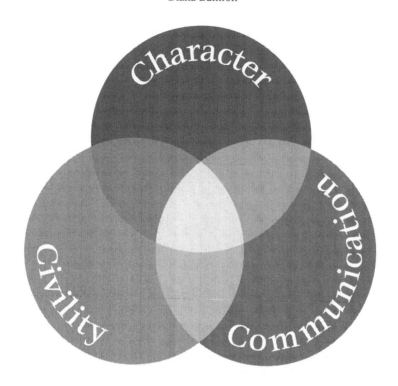

"You *Communicate* your *Character* by how you exercise your *Civility*."

It became more and more obvious to me that our lives, personal and professional, are dependent on how we engage The 3 C's. Consider this:

You *Communicate* your *Character* by how you exercise your *Civility*. You and I are walking billboards for what we stand for in life. We each touch one another with our civility or incivility. That incivility can spark from indifference, lack of awareness, and ignorance. Incivility can spring out of frustration or confusion. Misplaced loyalty can give birth to incivility. It can, however, also be intentional, arising from retaliation or narcissism. No matter its source, incivility harms, erodes, and destroys. I'm not referring just to the people you and I touch with our incivility. I'm referring to *us*. When we are not focused and relentless about our own civility, we begin to slowly eat away at our own core—our character.

The 3 C's approach underscores that Civility, Communication, and Character are interdependent. Like individual links in a chain, rather than being independent of one another, they are very much dependent on one another. Each C affects the other two C's—and they're only as strong as the weakest link. As I just mentioned, incivility eats away at character. Be rude and inconsiderate enough, and your character will begin to erode. Poor communication skills lead to incivility quickly, and exceptional communication skills can demonstrate civility—which in turn, remember, can strengthen your character. Like the diagram shows, The 3 C's are interdependent. Ignore any of them, and the other two will weaken. Strengthen one, and the other two will become more robust.

This book focuses on one element of The 3 C's: civility. I want you to embrace the concept of civility, its value, and that the responsibility for civility isn't with the other guy. It's with you! Civility is your responsibility!

Civility in the workplace isn't to be just considered, it's to be demanded—from ourselves as well as from others. It's the lack of civility born out of fear, ignorance, confusion, or malice that creates the hostile workplace. But the good news is that there are steps that you and I can take to detect the first clues of toxicity, begin the eradication of a harmful work environment, and create one that is civil and respectful. There are also steps that you and I can take to protect ourselves and become positive influences for others if we are caught in the snares of an ugly workplace.

Although a toxic work environment took a toll on me, I don't for a minute think I was a total innocent. Had I taken some of the steps I recommend in this book, I would have put myself in a far stronger position to influence myself toward a point of strength as well as more positively influence others caught in the grasp of the toxicity.

Although incivility can look like an explosion—furious outbursts, slammed doors, humiliating public put-downs, or vicious emails—you (yes, you!) can introduce civility by planting mere seeds. You may not be in the position of instituting a major policy for a shift in culture. Yet you are, however, in the position to nurture civility in your environment in your own small ways.

It takes desire, commitment, and energy. If you're a leader who wants to influence from a position of civility and respect, but you don't know how, please keep reading. If you see the first signs of bad behavior creeping into a good workplace, I invite you to keep turning the pages. And if you're a target of rudeness, disrespect, or cruel behavior, you've come to the right place. You are not alone. Please consider me your companion as you read through this book. I know how you feel, and I want to help you through the lessons I've learned from my experience, interviews, and research. Please tuck this book into a spot where you can grab it for a nudge or an idea of encouragement.

I provide research, case studies, and steps to help you in this endeavor. I also changed names to protect the innocent, the guilty, and the guilty who think they're innocent. But more than all else, I wish for you to be part of a workplace that is healthy and positive. In other words, one that is civil!

This book is broken into four parts:

- **Part I** is an overview of civility.
- **Part II** investigates what it takes to be a civil business and shows that a business that holds civility in high esteem finds rewards in its employees.
- **Part III** explores what it takes to be a civil leader and how to become one.
- **Part IV** examines what it means to be civil to oneself. If we're not civil to ourselves, it's very difficult to be civil to others.

Finally, throughout the book, I provide **Civility Wrap-ups** of each chapter. You are responsible for your own civility. It's also up to you to determine what and how you contribute to your workplace. Please use my **Civility Wrap-ups** as tools to contribute civility. I also ask you to **C's the Day** in these opportunities to clearly define your next moves.

You and I have this wonderful opportunity, and believe me, we need it more than ever. Our families, our society, our workplaces need civility. Here we go! We're going to...

Unleash Civility!

NOTES INTRODUCTION

1   Friedrich Nietzsche, "The Twilight of the Idols; or How to Philosophize with a Hammer" in *The Works of Friedrich Nietzsche*, Vol. XI (New York: Macmillan & Co., 1896).

2   Christine Pearson and Christine Porath, *The Cost of Bad Behavior: How Incivility Is Damaging Your Business and What to Do about It* (New York: Portfolio, 2009).

PART I: CIVILITY 101

CHAPTER 1
The Force of Civility

When *New York Times* readers turned to the editorial page on March 14, 2012, they probably were not anticipating finding a stunning column written by an executive of the financial giant Goldman Sachs announcing his resignation.

With no warning, Greg Smith told the world he'd had enough. Smith's editorial had described the company's environment as the most toxic and destructive that he'd ever seen. According to the now former exec, Goldman Sachs' culture of trust—what he called "the secret sauce that made this place great and allowed us to earn our clients' trust for 143 years"—had evaporated and been replaced by a culture of greed.[1]

Imagine for a moment that you're a client of Goldman Sachs. You're sipping your triple shot mocha, you pull up the *Times'* editorial page, and you read that five different managing directors of Goldman Sachs referred to their own clients as "Muppets," not only in conversations, but also through in-house email.[2] That $5 cup of coffee is now in your lap, and you're wondering whether you're Kermit the Frog or Miss Piggy.

In dollars and cents, that editorial depicting distrust, disrespect, and despicable behavior at the financial giant took an enormous toll. The next day, Goldman Sachs saw $2.15 billion of its market value disintegrate with shares dropping 3.4 percent.[3] Goldman Sachs paid a huge price financially for its tolerance of incivility, but the toll caused by that permissiveness went further than the bottom line. In not only Goldman Sachs, but in corporations and organizations worldwide, incivility leaves in its wake ruined reputations, broken relationships, and shattered teams. In our too-big-to-fail society, the stock price may bounce back, but trusting relationships do not.

You may be thinking, "Goldman Sachs wasn't a case of incivility!" I beg to differ. Toxic environments don't just materialize. They are created. They are the product of an attitude that is tolerant, permissive, and yes, even encouraging of incivility. The business that turns the other way when disrespect begins to creep in invites a culture of failure. Leadership, at every level, might as well roll out the welcome mat to toxic behavior if it overlooks insolence, gossip, and rudeness. Written policies are worthless in the maintenance of a healthy and civil environment if impertinence and impolite behavior go unchecked.

When our businesses, organizations, educational institutions, and governmental agencies ignore the first instances of incivility, it's not long before people become targets of rudeness, victims of vicious gossip, and objects of intentional undermining: recipients of uncivil behavior. Ignoring civility feeds incivility: offenders crank up rudeness, gossip gets the go-ahead, and bullying grows. Incivility is like a cancer. Unless it's immediately addressed, it's not long before the entire body is in pain and weakened.

If your business is not planting and nurturing seeds of civility as well as weeding out incivility quickly and unapologetically, it's being set up for a toxic environment to take root. Teams that don't trust each other, leaders who don't demonstrate respect, and an environment plagued by anger, rudeness, and fear are the rewards for looking the other way when incivility begins to creep into an organization.

If you think that the financial repercussions of incivility are unique to a huge corporation like Goldman Sachs, think again. Research shows that incivility costs American businesses between $300 and $360 billion a year.[4] Look around your business. Each individual that you see, whether a long-standing leader or a brand-new worker, is costing the company thousands of dollars if incivility is feathering its nest in your workplace. Team members who aren't communicating, connecting, or demonstrating mutual respect wrack up a financial toll quickly. Cha-ching! How long can any business operate with that kind of ongoing erosion of the bottom line?

CIVILITY ENSURES YOUR COMPANY'S HEALTH

Civility is indispensable to the success of your business. It's essential to the financial and emotional health of your company. It's a non-negotiable for your employees. Civility is crucial to your brand's reputation.

Maintaining civility is no easy task. After all, we're talking about behavior—how people treat one another. One minute a professional environment can be cohesive and productive, and in a matter of days or weeks, all those positive feelings can be turned upside down. A new employee may enter the scene, perhaps there is a change in leadership, or assigned responsibilities change or increase. A personal matter such as a divorce, illness, or financial setback can affect a colleague in such a negative manner that anger, frustration, or fear are new additions to the atmosphere.

Incivility can make its debut in all forms of behavior—sometimes overt, often subtle. Here are some examples of blatant, and not-so-blatant incivility, that you may experience (or even display) in the workplace (or in other settings).

Blatant Incivility

- Rolling your eyes at someone's suggestion
- Showing up late
- Interrupting conversations
- Imposing yourself and your opinions in others' discussions
- Reacting with anger or disgust
- Criticizing someone in public
- Making sarcastic remarks
- Cracking inappropriate jokes at the expense of others
- Belittling or putting others down and name calling
- Yelling

Subtle Incivility

- Disappearing when it's time to do your job
- Making personal calls on company time
- Not responding to communication
- Responding poorly to communication
- Blaming others
- Taking the credit for others' work
- Not holding yourself and others accountable
- Leading inconsistently—no one is on the same page
- Playing favorites
- Leading by proxy—you do the easy leading, and hand off the more difficult responsibilities to others
- Exhibiting unpredictable behavior—it's all unicorns and roses one day, zombies and poison ivy the next
- Being undependable
- Violating dress codes
- Gossiping
- Using company computers and other technology for personal use
- Allowing toxic employees and leaders to unleash their misery and negativity with no repercussions

The problem with incivility is that we're quick to point the finger at the other person; we're quick to criticize *their* incivility. Yet it's impossible to change someone else's behavior (as any parent of teenagers can tell you). All we can do is change ourselves and how we react to a given situation. As you read these pages, I want to focus on *you!* Your civility and yes, your incivility. Let's face it, we all have our moments when we rudely interrupt, sound condescending or sarcastic, or fail to pick up on the fact that we have just embarrassed or angered another person because of our behavior.

Sometimes, we're just plain oblivious. We neither take the time to pay attention nor have we cultivated our sense of awareness. We're zeroed in on *ourselves*. When it's all about *us*, we've set the stage for incivility. So how do we eradicate it? By focusing on civility. And that means focusing on others.

CIVILITY DEFINED

Civility is the consistent implementation of respect. It's how you regularly and continually communicate kindness, thoughtfulness, and respect through your words, body language, and behavior.

Here's the catch—civility takes work. It takes awareness. And it takes practice!

Just like sticking with a diet or maintaining an exercise regimen, civility requires discipline. The determination it takes to resist a piece of chocolate cheesecake is exactly the same type of resolve necessary when you want to bark at your colleague whose recommendation you think is absolutely absurd...and don't. The self-discipline necessary to wake up and jog three miles every morning is the same self-discipline needed to take the time to respectfully and clearly respond to communication. Civility depends on self-control; incivility is the product of a lack of control.

Too often organizations, businesses—and all of us in them—are civil and respectful when everything runs smoothly. But when the pressure's on and we need civility more than ever, the self-discipline necessary to engage with civility seems too demanding; that's when we give up on civility and it's game over.

Although we tend to think that what prompts uncivil behavior by others is a stressful workplace, often rude behavior is triggered by what's happening on a personal level.

Civility depends on self-control; incivility is the product of a lack of control.

Walking on Eggshells

Henry was in charge of a governmental agency responsible for helping citizens walk through the demands of rules and regulations. His employees spent their days telling taxpayers, "No, your paperwork is insufficient," "Your paperwork isn't filled out correctly," and "Your paperwork requires a fee." In other words, for the most part, the employees delivered bad news to people who were already frustrated and unhappy. Despite the less than perfect conditions, the agency's employees endeavored to be as helpful and thorough as possible. In the best of conditions this wasn't an easy job, but it was made more difficult by Henry's mercurial and inconsistent attitude. When everything was going well at home, Henry arrived with smiles and showered his staff with compliments, appreciation, and gentle reminders. When his home life was less than ideal, Henry's team knew it. He barked orders, was quick to point the finger at others, and shut himself behind closed doors. The inconsistency was untenable, and turnover was fast and furious.

THE CIVILITY: TRUST CONNECTION

The demand for a civil culture is no fluffy, cookie-cutter approach coming down as the latest corporate get-along plan. There is nothing about civility that is artificial or cookie-cutter. Civility takes work, it takes skill, and it takes patience. That work, those skills, and your patience are essential to build an environment that is civil and shows respect for others—whether or not you agree with those "others." Work, skill, and patience are ingredients that lead to a culture of trust.

Civility doesn't look or sound the same in every organization. You would no more expect behavior at a construction site to resemble that of a bank or the rules for football to apply to a swim meet.

Here's the bottom line: civility is about respect, whether or not you agree with the person, whether or not that person is your leader or your direct report, no matter whether you even *like* the person! Your job is to learn the language of respect—that language is civility.

If you've been in a country where you don't know the language, you know that it's more difficult to navigate, check off anything on your "to do" list, and distinguish between a joke, a compliment, or an insult. You can certainly get by without knowing the language and understanding the culture, but the trek takes longer, is more doubtful, and can include unwanted detours when you're unsure. It's unfamiliar and it's uncomfortable. Everything runs more smoothly when you understand the lingo and the culture surrounding those words.

It's no different in an organization. When people speak the same language (that of civility) and understand the culture (one built on respect), trust grows, cooperation prospers, and engagement results.

When I'm called in to help companies take their workplace from toxic to trusting, it's nearly always a matter of looking at the not-so-civil culture. In many ways, every company is identical:

- Everyone wants to be treated with civility.
- There are some folks who don't necessarily want to take the time and make the effort to treat others with civility.

More often than not, everyone is speaking their own language of civility. The result is cacophony.

However, when a company is willing to make the commitment to civility, when everyone is speaking the same language of civility, it can sound like a symphony...as you'll see in chapter 2. But before heading there, let's do a quick **Civility Wrap-up** and then close out the chapter with how you will **C's the Day**!

Civility Wrap-Up

- Civility is the consistent implementation of respect.

- It's a culture of civility that builds a foundation for trust.

- U.S. companies are losing $300 to $360 billion every year because of stress, and much of that stems from workplace incivility.[6]

- There is no cookie cutter approach to civility.

- Civility depends on self-control!

C's the Day

This is *your* commitment to creating a civil culture. Look at the lists of blatant and subtle incivility on the preceding pages.

1. What examples of incivility can you add to these lists from your own workplace?

2. How about you? Could you be doing something or *not* doing something that makes the workplace just a bit (or a lot) more uncivil?

3. Now write down three changes that you can make immediately to start sowing the seeds to introduce, increase, or reinforce civility in yourself and in your organization's culture.

Communicating Character by Exercising Civility

NOTES CHAPTER 1

1   Greg Smith, "Why I Am Leaving Goldman Sachs," *New York Times*, March 14, 2012, www.nytimes.com/2012/03/14/opinion/why-i-am-leaving-goldman-sachs.html.

2   Ibid.

3   Christine Harper, "Goldman Roiled by Op-Ed Loses $2.2 Billion," Bloomberg Business, March 15, 2012, www.bloomberg.com/news/articles/2012-03-15/goldman-stunned-by-op-ed-loses-2-2-billion-for-shareholders.

4   Christine Pearson and Christine Porath, *The Cost of Bad Behavior: How Incivility Is Damaging Your Business and What to Do About It* (New York: Portfolio, 2009), 4; David K. Williams, "How Much Do Bad Bosses Cost American Businesses?" Forbes.com, September 24, 2012, www.forbes.com/sites/davidkwilliams/2012/09/24/how-much-do-bad-bosses-cost-american-businesses.

5   Christine Pearson and Christine Porath, *The Cost of Bad Behavior: How Incivility Is Damaging Your Business and What to Do About It* (New York: Portfolio, 2009), 4.

CHAPTER 2
Civility's Influence on Corporate Culture

Imagine driving to your favorite grocery store and finding that the employees aren't inside the store, but rather are in the parking lot picketing. They're holding signs urging you not to shop at their place of employment. A union strike? No. They're demanding the return of their beloved CEO. This really happened in 2014 when the employees of Demoulas Market Basket, one of the most successful family-owned grocery store chains in New England, walked off the job. CEO Arthur T. Demoulas had been ousted by his own cousin, Arthur S. Demoulas, and a new board of directors in an ugly family battle for company control.[1] (Obviously, the Demoulas differences went beyond their middle initials!)

Thousands of employees flocked to Market Basket's headquarters and local stores not to check in for work, but to demand the return of the leader who, they said, treated them like family. All employees risked losing their paychecks—some were fired—as they refused to work for the new board that dumped the man these employees considered "the epitome of what a CEO should be."[2] Likewise, huge numbers of customers took their business elsewhere, a rejection of the new change at the helm.

WALKING THE TALK

What was the force that moved employees to risk their jobs, managers to jeopardize their status, and customers to change their shopping habits? At the heart of those actions was loyalty based on the powerful force of civility exhibited to all by one Arthur T. Demoulas.

Demoulas treated his employees and his customers with kindness, thoughtfulness, and respect. And this is no small collection of corner markets. Market Basket includes 71 stores that employ 25,000 workers. Demoulas remembered his employees' names, no matter their job or how long they'd been with the company. He showed that civility actually had a feel to it whenever he reached out, hugged an employee, and asked about a sick family member.

For Demoulas, civility went far beyond courtesy. He thought his employees should earn more and that his customers should pay less, and he made his ideas a reality. When it came time for job promotions, he focused on advancement from within. His community of customers and employees fought for him because he demonstrated respect for each employee, whether the employee was a cashier, truck driver, or store manager. Demoulas' shoppers felt his respect no matter how much they spent at the check-out stand.

Demoulas had made civility an indisputable ingredient of his brand. As a result, at a time when 88 percent of employees had little or no passion for their work, the employees and management of Demoulas Market Basket risked everything to fight for the man they wanted back at the top.[3] If that's not passion, what is?

After being reinstated as CEO, Demoulas told his supporters at a rally in celebration of his return, "You have demonstrated to the world that it is a person's moral obligation and social responsibility to protect a culture which provides an honorable and a dignified place in which to work."[4]

Before you claim that Demoulas' employees weren't moved by respect so much as by dollars and benefits, let me be very clear—more money in a paycheck can have a huge effect. But remember, at the celebratory rally for him, Demoulas talked about the protection of the *culture* of Market Basket.

CORPORATE CULTURE UNLEASHED

A culture is about more than wages. In terms of an organization, *culture* is defined by Merriam-Webster as "the set of shared attitudes, values, goals, and practices that characterizes an institution or organization."[5]

Demoulas was very clear about the Demoulas Market Basket culture; his definition included the financial well-being of his employees *and* his customers. But it wasn't enough to pay his men and women what he thought they deserved. Demoulas spoke his own language of civility when he reached out with a smile, gave a hug of support, and expressed interest in the individual.

Assessing Your Culture and Your Role in It

Stop for a moment and look around:

- Are you protecting a culture that honors people and treats individuals, no matter their position or role, with dignity?
- What type of culture *are* you protecting?
- Even if you're not a leader and you don't think that you're in a position to create change, do you take personal responsibility for your own civility?
- If you are a leader, would your followers describe you as "the epitome of what a CEO should be"?

When working with companies, I find that when people begin to answer these questions honestly, they take the first steps of transformation with a far keener sense of awareness and perception.

 "The deepest principle of human nature is the craving to be appreciated." —William James

Appreciation Is Key

The Father of American Psychology, William James, said that "the deepest principle of human nature is the craving to be appreciated." Referring to James' quote, management über-guru Tom Peters says that,

> I have long thought that those are among the most profound words I've ever stumbled upon. For I do fervently believe that appreciation is indeed the most powerful force of nature and

hence, practically speaking, the premier 'motivational tool' available to bosses-managers-leaders (not to mention parents and teachers and spouses).[6]

Like Peters, Demoulas understood the effect that appreciation has on everyone in an environment of gratitude. In our fast-paced, technologically driven workplaces, appreciation is too often overlooked as a time-suck—an act that many consider unnecessary, superficial, perhaps, even uncomfortable. Appreciation is a component of civility that energizes and makes the recipient of that praise feel more firmly planted in the workplace. Civility's component of appreciation is powerful, yet often it's overlooked, forgotten, or rejected. We don't understand that appreciation is expressed by saying two words that we don't say often enough: *thank you.*

American businessman, writer, and former CEO of Herman Miller, Inc. Max De Pree said, "The first responsibility of a leader is to define reality. The last is to say thank you. In between, the leader is a servant."[7] *Thank you* is the sound of humility and appreciation.

APPRECIATION ASSESSMENT

Time to check out just how comfortable you are expressing appreciation to others. Please take a moment to answer the following questions. Score each Always with 5 points, each Sometimes with 3 points, and each Never with 0 points. Of the 17 questions, there's the potential for a low score of 0 (You've got some work to do!) and a high score of 85 (You're a Jedi Master of Appreciation!). Thanks!

If You're a Leader

I show appreciation to my employees and customers.	Always	Sometimes	Never
It's natural for me to say, "Thanks, great job," or "Thanks for coming in."	Always	Sometimes	Never
I make time to express appreciation.	Always	Sometimes	Never
I think leaders should express appreciation to build a civil workplace.	Always	Sometimes	Never
I know how to express appreciation to people.	Always	Sometimes	Never

If You're a Manager

I show appreciation to my direct reports, customers, and leaders.	Always	Sometimes	Never
I show appreciation by doing nice things for my employees from time to time.	Always	Sometimes	Never
I show appreciation to my leaders, even if they make more than I do.	Always	Sometimes	Never
I appreciate when staff and customers point out shortfalls and problems.	Always	Sometimes	Never
I make time to express appreciation.	Always	Sometimes	Never
I know how to express appreciation to people.	Always	Sometimes	Never

If You're a Direct Report

I show appreciation to my colleagues, customers, managers, and leaders.	Always	Sometimes	Never
I feel it's my job to express appreciation.	Always	Sometimes	Never
I think my customers appreciate when I offer good service.	Always	Sometimes	Never
I think my manager sees my appreciation as genuine.	Always	Sometimes	Never
I make time to express appreciation.	Always	Sometimes	Never
I know how to express appreciation to people.	Always	Sometimes	Never

How did you do? Did you find that the magic words of appreciation come easily? Or could it be that *thank you* is an estranged friend in your workplace and you need to brush up on your gratitude skills?

Appreciation must be part of your culture. Granted you may not have the financial wherewithal to cut employees bigger paychecks or provide increasing benefits, but that is no excuse for not including appreciation. Time and time again, employees tell me that when their managers, their supervisors, their leaders thank them for a job well done, they feel that they're contributing to the culture. You should see their faces as they describe the effect of that new found appreciation—often, they're grinning ear to ear. No matter your job in any organization, you can have a tremendous effect by adding *thank you* and by showing true appreciation for a job well done. I'm not asking you to do anything that is superficial, but when a colleague has helped you in some way, watch what a sprinkle of appreciation will do to your relationship with that person.

When you exercise civility through appreciation, you show that you care about another human being. You actually begin to make a personal connection, an increasing rarity in these days of technology, social media, and rudeness.

When exposed to Demoulas' display of appreciation, people felt a force at work, and his choice to exercise that force unleashed a power that made a difference in the lives of those who worked for him and therefore in the business itself.

Demoulas is the perfect example of **The 3 C's** principle. Demoulas **Communicated his Character**—who he is at his core—**by how he exercised his Civility**—how he treated his employees and customers.

THE DIFFERENCE A *THANK YOU* MAKES

In the small yet influential book *The Power of Small*, authors Linda Kaplan Thaler and Robin Koval describe the turnover issues confronting the New York law firm Sullivan & Cromwell. For two years, the firm watched as 30 percent of its lawyers walked away. Salaries too small? No! Kaplan Thaler and Koval say the attorneys were extremely well paid and had great benefits. Promotions weren't even a problem. However, appreciation was.

"When the journal *American Lawyer* published its annual review of midlevel associates, Sullivan & Cromwell ranked near the very bottom of 163 firms surveyed."[8]

In 2006, two phrases began showing up on a regular basis: *please* and *thank you*. Now, the senior partners began to punctuate their conversations with these phrases that showed appreciation and value. They replaced curt demands with politeness and requests. Their appreciation also included praising the young attorneys for their work. Although the firm didn't spend any money on this addition to its culture, the results were priceless.

"When the next *American Lawyer* review rolled around, Sullivan & Cromwell was rated the *top* employer among New York firms."[9] Adding *please* and *thank you*, taking the time to show appreciation, and including politeness in the language created a shift in culture. That shift was away from an atmosphere of "command and follow" and toward "lead and trust."

In the next chapter, we'll take a look at the contagious behavior of incivility and how it can submarine your brand. But let's first take a look at the **Civility Wrap-up** and then close out this chapter with how you can **C's the Day**!

Civility Wrap-Up

- "The deepest principle of human nature is the craving to be appreciated." –William James

- "The premier motivational tool is *appreciation.*" –Tom Peters

- Adding *please* and *thank you* to your corporate culture costs nothing but adds tremendous value to each member of your business community.

C's the Day

I appreciate your wanting to get to the next chapter, but please pause a few moments. (Notice I added two signals of appreciation here: *appreciate* and *please.*)

1. Flip back to the Appreciation Assessment. Review your responses to each question. For each Sometimes and Never you picked, write down what your difficulty is and how you can increase your appreciation of the people around you.

2. Write down your role in your organization.

3. Would your peers, colleagues, direct reports, or managers describe you as the epitome of that role? If not, why not?

Communicating Character by Exercising Civility

NOTES CHAPTER 2

1 Callum Borchers, "Arthur T. Demoulas's Personal Touch Can Cut Both Ways," *Boston Globe*, August 22, 2014, www.bostonglobe.com/business/2014/08/21/arthur-demoulas-profile-personal-touch-that-can-cut-two-ways/IqkmJ1i7A4AFKpLenN8vBM/story.html.

2 "2014," We Are Market Basket, http://wearemarketbasket.com/2014/12/.

3 Jeff Fermin, "13 Disturbing Facts about Employee Engagement," [Infographic] Huffpost Business, November 13, 2014, www.huffingtonpost.com/jeff-fermin/13-disturbing-facts-about_b_6140996.html.

4 Alana Semuels, "Power to the Workers: How Grocery Chain Employees Saved Beloved CEO," *Los Angeles Times*, August 28, 2014, www.latimes.com/nation/nationnow/la-na-nn-market-basket-ceo-arthur-t-demoulas-20140828-story.html.

5 Merriam-Webster's Collegiate Dictionary, 11th ed., s.v. "culture."

6 Tom Peters, "Dispatches from the New World of Work," www.tompeters.com/dispatches/011351.php (page discontinued).

7 Max De Pree, BrainyQuote.com, Xplore Inc. (2015), www.brainyquote.com/quotes/quotes/m/maxdepree100557.html.

8 Linda Kaplan Thaler and Robin Koval, *The Power of Small* (New York: Broadway, 2009), 36–37.

9 Ibid.

CHAPTER 3
Incivility: The Dark Side of Bad Behavior

"You underestimate the power of the Dark Side." When Darth Vader, wielding his light saber, said these words to Luke Skywalker, little did the business world know that the villainous cyborg was warning it about the costs of incivility. Okay, maybe the issue of incivility in the workplace was not exactly what George Lucas had in mind, but the fact is that incivility *is* the dark side of human behavior, and we *do* underestimate its power.

> *Incivility* is *the dark side of human behavior, and we* do *underestimate its power.*

Like civility, incivility is a force that affects everyone in its path. Unlike civility, absolutely nothing good comes from incivility. The problem is that too often incivility is not recognized for what it is before the damage has been done. After all, incivility doesn't enter with a flourish wearing a black cape, helmet, and full face mask. Perhaps, if it did, it would be immediately deleted at first sight. Instead, it tiptoes in through seemingly inconsequential missteps:

- The hurried email in all caps that reads as though the Wicked Witch of the West pressed send
- Ongoing interruptions at meetings because we just don't have time (*...to listen*)
- The rolling of the eyes at a suggestion (*Oh, stop being so sensitive!*)

- The ongoing delays to respond to requests that hinder the ability to proceed (*I'll get to it...don't be so impatient.*)
- The impatience with customers (*They ask such stupid questions.*)
- The impatience with colleagues (*They ask such stupid questions.*)
- The impatience with management (*They ask such stupid questions.*)
- The inability to make eye contact with a human being because our eyes are glued to some smart technical device (*Hey, it's important to follow what's happening on Twitter.*)

Maybe there's a chance that you and I have been guilty of one or two of the above actions or inactions as well. After all, we're only human and are capable of making mistakes every now and then. However, if you witness these behaviors *often* in your office—or even cop to doing them yourself—tread carefully. The seeds of incivility are already taking root. Potentially dangerous raw emotions of anger, hatred, aggression, and jealousy lead to interactions that can create an internal momentum of feelings that is anything but conducive to trusting relationships, personal or professional. Our negative attitudes of others' differences, whether those differences are of culture, age, gender, politics, religion, life experiences, you name it, become a springboard to generate an even greater build-up of negative emotions. And then when those negative emotions are what influence behavior, watch out! Incivility just got the green light.

When we allow incivility, wrapped in our actions and inactions, to slither into our businesses and our lives, we allow it to begin redefining everything about us and our business. Incivility takes the reins, and it's not long before it takes control. We permit incivility to control our communication and our behavior.

A Flame Spreads Quickly

Theresa is helping a customer with a purchase when her manager, Mr. Cranky Pants, walks over. In front of the customer, Mr. Cranky Pants begins to reprimand Theresa for failing to handle some merchandise as he had instructed earlier that morning. Theresa is speechless. Her customer looks down, obviously uncomfortable with the one-sided exchange. Mr. Cranky Pants walks off in a huff, and Theresa quietly concludes her business with the customer. Embarrassed, she bids her customer adieu.

And now it begins! The fallout of incivility, Theresa's internal dialogue sounds something like this:

- *Why* did that just happen? *Because my manager is an idiot!*
- *Why does he always do that? Because he hates me, and he's an idiot!*

Theresa begins to identify the manager as the opposition, not a leader who instructs and supports. How does that lead to productive and professional behavior? Or perhaps, her internal self-talk goes something like this:

- *Why* did this just happen? *Because I deserve it. I'm such a flake.*
- *Why* does he always do that? *Because I don't do anything right.*

Now, Theresa begins to identify herself as a victim.

Both conclusions are ugly. Whether Theresa identifies the manager as her opponent or herself as a flake, she has set herself up to be less productive, less loyal, and less effective. She loses and the company loses.

And the customer? Even if the employee manages to shake off the public attack, the customer comes up with her own image of the company—and it's probably not the branding the company's marketing department had in mind.

No doubt, the bewildered customer is asking herself similar questions.

- *What* was that all about?
- *What* did that kid do to deserve being unloaded on in front of me...*the customer?*
- *What* kind of company would allow such obnoxious, rude treatment of its employees by its managers?

INCIVILITY IS CONTAGIOUS

A company's reputation is more fragile than ever. Writing for Forbes. com, Alexander F. Brigham and Stefan Linssen report that in just 30 years, intangible assets have replaced the tangible when it comes to value.[1] It used to be that nearly 100 percent of a corporation's value was in tangible assets; today that number has dropped to about 25 percent. Three quarters of the average corporation's value is intangible. "In other words, a business's most valuable asset is its good name, its brand and reputation."[2]

After Theresa's manager barked at her in front of her customer, that customer, no doubt, had a less than positive image of the store and its brand. If you think it's no big deal since we're talking about the effect on *one customer*, think again.

Incivility can sink a brand. When you and I witness incivility, it leaves its mark, and it's not good. You don't have to be the victim of disrespectful, callous behavior for incivility to make a negative impression. When incivility strikes, people talk. Just watching rude behavior, whether it's colleague to colleague, employee to client, or customer to employee, prompts observers to repeat the ugly tale to friends and family. People are so turned off by incivility that they spread the word.

Research conducted by Christine Pearson and Christine Porath found that more than half of the people who *witnessed* incivility between employees and other customers no longer felt quite so friendly toward the company.[3] We're not talking about experiencing incivility here; we're talking about the effects of *witnessing* it. Customers often talk with their feet—and their keyboards—and will shun establishments they feel are unfriendly. It only takes seconds to permanently flame something online with a bad review or rating.

Businesses ignore incivility at their own peril. Incivility's effect is so strong that buying habits change. Half of the individuals surveyed said that after witnessing incivility, in the future, they wouldn't do business with the company. Businesses take huge risks if they think a singular incident of rudeness observed by one person won't amount to anything—research indicates otherwise. More than 80 percent of the people who saw another individual treated disrespectfully, whether the target was an employee or customer, talked! So-called short-lived singular incidents of uncivil behavior aren't so short-lived when talk keeps the episode alive.

Lest we forget, people aren't talking only person to person, by phone, or by email these days. Social media is the fastest way to build or destroy a reputation. *#Incivility* is not the hashtag you want to see referring to your business or to you.

Witnessing Incivility

- 83 percent of people surveyed described the uncivil treatment they witnessed to a friend or family member.
- 55 percent adopted a less favorable attitude toward the company where they witnessed incivility in action.
- 50 percent of people were less willing to use the company's products and services.

—Christine Pearson and Christine Porath, *The Cost of Bad Behavior*

WHY THE NEGATIVE BEHAVIOR?

Why did Theresa's boss blister her in front of a customer? Why did he go after her in such a rude manner? Who knows? Perhaps *his* superior had just dumped on him in front of one of his own direct reports. Maybe his wife filed for divorce, and he learned about it over breakfast. It may be that he just missed his morning espresso. Unless this dark side of behavior is addressed quickly, it will continue to take a toll.

You and I each react to people, conversations, and situations differently. Take a moment to think about the last time you drove around your town running errands. Now picture this scenario: you see the upcoming traffic light turn yellow. You and the drivers around you display different reactions to the same event:

- One driver takes his foot off the accelerator a football field away from the intersection.

- A second motorist floors it.
- The third (obviously you) continues to drive at the posted speed limit.

Here are the conditions of what could be happening in the other drivers' cars:

- One driver doesn't even notice the light change because he is preoccupied with texting or changing the radio station.
- Another driver doesn't notice the light change because she's turned around yelling at her kids in the back seat.
- Yet another driver might notice the light but blows through it anyway because he is using the rear view mirror to check his hair.

You and I each react to the inanimate caution light differently. Our moods, our personalities, our deadlines, our surroundings, and our perceptions all affect our reactions. So imagine that if a predictable traffic indicator prompts various reactions—some positive, many not so positive—what happens when we deal with other human beings and their emotions?

NEGATIVE TRIGGERS AND HOT BUTTONS

Just about any conversation about incivility in the workplace will include the words *trigger* and *hot buttons*. "My manager knows Mitchell's hot buttons, and knows how to push them." "Every time Jack walks in late, I want to scream!" "Rosa knows that when she interrupts me in meetings, she's going to trigger some confrontation." I'm sure you may have a couple of your own hot buttons or negative triggers.

A *trigger* is defined as anything, as an act or event that serves as a stimulus and initiates or precipitates a reaction or series of reactions.[4] In non-dictionary language, a trigger is something that would, in our case, ignite incivility.

Although a trigger is something that can produce a reaction in most of us (such as that co-worker who constantly interrupts everyone midsentence), a hot button is specific to an individual. Because of some past experience, you have a unique reaction to an event, action, or a situation that would not affect nearly anyone else. Although you consider your colleagues' questions about your elderly mother's health as caring and thoughtful, when Carmen asks you, you cringe. You know that no matter how you respond, Carmen will respond with one dire prediction after another.

Hot buttons are always negative. Although triggers can be positive or negative, I'm going to focus on negative triggers that can provoke incivility. Both hot buttons and negative triggers refer to anything that causes people to feel strong emotions—fear, anger, frustration, suspicion. The negative stimulus can be an act or event, but it can also be a mere observation—seeing that certain someone who evokes mental wincing at their very sight. Negative triggers and hot buttons ignite incivility.

Each of us has different triggers and hot buttons. What makes all of this even more complicated for us is that what's a trigger for us one day may not be a trigger to spark our less-than-civil reaction the next. That inconsistency holds true for others as well. Think of that colleague who welcomes your feedback one day and the next day snarls that you're always criticizing.

Triggers, like hot buttons, are emotional! Recognizing your own emotional instigators begins the process of learning how to respond to them, which is the first step in exercising civility. Can you relate to any of these triggers?

Social Media

There's something about anonymity that sparks rampant incivility on social media. Maybe it's not having to look an individual in the eye, or maybe it's the same internal cheerleader that urges us to gun it at that yellow light. Obscenity-laden derisive comments may be evidence that we enjoy freedom of speech, but it doesn't do much to encourage civil discourse—and it's a heck of a way to kick-start your day.

Engaging in social media can spark negativity even without nasty comments. For example, you've been waiting days for a colleague or friend to respond to your recent voice mail or email. You've not heard one word from them. But then you check Facebook, and look who's posting? Your missing colleague. Your reaction? *She has the time to post, but can't find the time to get back to me?* See what I mean? Social media can be a trigger for incivility.

Research shows that posting too many selfies can damage relationships, and seeing too much good news from friends who post about their perfect lives can leave you feeling deflated.[5]

Emotional contagion can take place through technological networks. In case you're wondering whether social media can infiltrate your emotions, consider the reported manipulation by Facebook. For one week in 2012 Facebook skewed news feeds of 700,000 users to provoke positive or negative responses.[6] Apparently, you and I can be swayed to add positive or negative comments depending on what's posted on our newsfeeds. According to an article by Andrew Griffin in the British newspaper *The Independent,* "Facebook manipulated the emotions of hundreds of thousands of its users, and found that they would pass on happy or sad emotions, it has said."[7]

If you want to start your day primed to make your workplace a better environment for teamwork, you may want to skip checking social media while sipping your morning beverage.

Public Reprimands

I admit that this is one of my major triggers. Public criticism is an ugly thing to experience or witness. It often prompts either silence by the target or an intense reaction that's angry and loud. Getting balled out in public by the boss, a colleague, or anyone can leave you feeling humiliated, stupid, and angry.

Seeing someone get flamed in public also has an effect on those who witness it. Just like the example of Theresa I used earlier, the customer left the store feeling ruffled and perplexed.

Let me be very clear here, I am not saying that you have only two choices when it comes to public reprimands: accept humiliation or take down the jerk who uttered them. There is a third option: deal with them through civility, which we'll delve into later in the book.

Snide Rhetorical Questions

The questions themselves are the triggers, and the responses are what you might want to say, but shouldn't. Nasty questions, especially from a supervisor, could be a trigger that requires your attention.

- "Do you know what your problem is?" (*I bet you're going to tell me.*)
- "Don't you remember?" (*If I remembered, would I ask you again?*)
- "Don't you ever get anything right?" (*Not when you're looking for everything I'm doing wrong.*)

Recognizing the trigger allows you to pause before making the next move.

Revenge Scenarios

Do you recognize this trigger? Revenge may work in the movies, but not in the workplace. When you've been undermined or treated rudely, it's easy to lose focus on your job and instead focus on how to get back at the offender. The last thing you need to do is to start the downward spiral of incivility by trying to get even through incivility, tempting as it may be.

Emotional Triggers

It's easy to say that the workplace would run more smoothly if we could just bar emotions, but the fact is that emotions are a huge part of who we are and what makes any business thrive. Most people will tell you that a positive work environment includes people filled with enthusiasm, excitement, happiness, inspiration, contentedness, strength, and eagerness. These emotions are the ingredients for not only a safe and satisfying business environment, but one that is successful and flourishing.

Too often, though, the emotions that take hold and spread throughout the workplace are negative: fear, anger, suspicion, jealousy, doubt, indifference, confusion, and disgust.

Emotional triggers that lead to negativity may be:

- **Jealousy.** Your boyfriend works at the same company as you, and you see him speak to another woman there.
- **Sarcasm.** Your colleague remarks, "Congrats! Nice job...for a new guy."
- **Personal remarks.** Comments about your personal features, like clothing style, weight, hair color or style, age, technical expertise.
- **Resentment.** You put in long hours for a project without any acknowledgment or thanks.

These are just some of the triggers that can launch incivility into action by blindsiding you. By recognizing which triggers prompt you to react either aggressively or rudely or with so much trepidation that you literally shut up and sit down, you begin to take the first steps to be the person who can transform the environment and make it healthier for *you!*

The trigger does not control the situation. It's the *reaction* to that trigger that has the power to escalate or de-escalate a negative condition in the workplace.

When leaders and employees learn to recognize triggers, they begin to define what makes an environment consistently civil. The result is a workplace that is safe emotionally as well as physically, and that builds the foundation for trust.

Pushing More Hot Buttons

Each person has his or her own hot buttons—maybe even an entire panel of buttons. We react immediately and without thought. Something said, a behavior, a political figure, a change in policy—there are so many possibilities! Actually, most of us share a lot of the same hot buttons. Knowing your own hot buttons and recognizing them for what they are puts you in a better place to deal with them *before* your button is pushed. Check the box next to the hot button issues that make you see red...please.

❑ Political discussions
❑ Religious discussions

- ❏ Tardiness
- ❏ Drivers who cut you off
- ❏ Being interrupted when speaking
- ❏ Being on hold...forever...by customer service
- ❏ Colleagues who are loud
- ❏ Explaining the same thing to a colleague more than once
- ❏ Personal phone calls on company time
- ❏ Micromanaging
- ❏ Personal questions—age, weight, etc.
- ❏ People checking their phones while you're talking

The American novelist and science fiction writer Robert Heinlein was onto something when he wrote, "A dying culture invariably exhibits personal rudeness. Bad manners. Lack of consideration in minor matters. A loss of politeness, of gentle manners, is more significant than is a riot."[8]

Understanding the force of incivility is vital in transforming an environment from toxic to trusting, but it takes more than understanding. It takes the action of you and me. Remember Mahatma Gandhi's words: You must be the change you wish to see in the world.[9]

In chapter 4, we'll see that the forces of both civility and incivility don't discriminate. They touch all of us within reach. We'll also see how your civility can make a difference in another's life, and not in the way you think. But before turning the page, please go through the **Civility Wrap-up** and finish this chapter with how you'll **C's the Day**!

Civility Wrap-Up

- Don't underestimate the power of incivility.

- The most important asset of your business is its good name.

- Most people who witness incivility spread the word.

- Half the people who see incivility eschew that company's goods and services.

- Become aware of your own *negative* triggers and hot buttons.

C's the Day

1. Awareness! Write down three personal triggers that launch you into negative emotions and poor behavior.

2. The next time those triggers materialize, what can you do differently so they don't have a negative effect on you?

3. Can you use social media differently to influence *you* more positively?

Communicating Character by Exercising Civility

NOTES CHAPTER 3

1 Alexander F. Brigham and Stefan Linssen, "Your Brand Reputational Value Is Irreplaceable. Protect It!" Forbes.com, February 1, 2010, www.forbes.com/2010/02/01/brand-reputation-value-leadership-managing-ethisphere.html.

2 Ibid.

3 Christine Pearson and Christine Porath, *The Cost of Bad Behavior: How Incivility Is Damaging Your Business and What to Do about It* (New York: Portfolio, 2009), 105.

4 Dictionary.com, s.v. "trigger."

5 Tracy Miller, "Too Many Selfies on Facebook Can Damage Relationships: Study," *New York Daily News,* August 12, 2013, www.nydailynews.com/life-style/selfies-damage-relationships-study-article-1.1424830; Ray Williams, "How Facebook Can Amplify Low Self-Esteem/Narcissism/Anxiety," *Psychology Today* (May 20, 2014), www.psychologytoday.com/blog/wired-success/201405/how-facebook-can-amplify-low-self-esteemnarcissismanxiety.

6 Andrew Griffin, "Facebook Manipulated Users' Moods in Secret Experiment," *The Independent,* June 29, 2014, www.independent.co.uk/life-style/gadgets-and-tech/facebook-manipulated-users-moods-in-secret-experiment-9571004.html.

7 Ibid.

8 Robert Heinlein, *Friday* (New York: Ballantine Books, 1982).

9 Mahatma Gandhi, BrainyQuote.com, Xplore Inc. (2015), www.brainyquote.com/quotes/quotes/m/mahatmagan109075.html.

CHAPTER 4
Civility: The Great Equalizer

"As human beings, our greatness lies not so much in being able to remake the world—that is the myth of the atomic age—as in being able to remake ourselves." —Mahatma Gandhi

Gandhi's words perfectly describe our unique responsibility and opportunity when it comes to civility. Too often we try to remake a colleague, boss, or client in the image of our concept of civility, when in fact, we only have the power to remake ourselves into an influence for civility. Our civility can become a force that affects everyone in its path.

A *force* is defined as a power to influence, affect, or control.[1] How you use that force determines your power to affect the life of a colleague, manager, or customer, which in turn affects the life of the business itself. Although we each have the opportunity to imprint a positive action on another person's experience, we often choose not to engage with the force of civility by making excuses: we don't have the time, we don't know how, and—even though we may not like to admit this one—we hide behind technology.

Consider the different forces of nature. Some forces lead to growth, healthful energy, and the nurturing of life itself. Mother Nature's gentle rains clean and purify. Here in Montana, our skies can be full of smoke from not only our state, but from blazes in other states as well. Only the rain is able to restore the skies to their smokeless condition so that we can, again, breathe deeply. Other forces leave in their wake destruction and even death.

When a hurricane plows though an area, nothing is left untouched. I grew up in South Florida and have experienced enough hurricanes to know that when you open the door (if that door is still on the hinges), and you survey the damage, you see that a hurricane does not differentiate between a mansion or a hut, a yacht or a dinghy, the rich or the poor. Its force doesn't strike one age group, one skin color, or one personality over another. It's a force that does not discriminate in any way.

Civility has that same effect—it's an equal opportunity force...but for good! Its consequence is not destructive, but positive, uplifting, and encouraging. Little in the path of civility is untouched by its respectful and courteous touch. Touched by civility, an associate is more productive, a team is more communicative, and a business is more profitable. The gale force winds of positive behavior spread more positive behavior.

RECOGNIZE THAT INCIVILITY IS INFECTIOUS

All too often this is exactly what happens in our businesses, our non-profit organizations, and our governmental agencies. The language of incivility is spoken through disrespectful and unpredictable behavior. When leadership permits unacceptable behavior by some at the expense of others, leaders not only tolerate disrespect, they embolden it.

Sometimes, we just don't want to catch what's going around. When I was in my twenties I had injured my thumb and ended up with an infection that spread to my hand and began to creep up my arm. It looked so nasty that even I didn't want to touch it. When shopping, I'd reach for the pen and credit card slip extended by the salesperson for me to sign. The salesperson would catch sight of my hand, and would quickly step back. They, obviously, were afraid they might "catch" whatever "ailed" me.

Afraid of "catching" the infection of nasty incivility in the workplace, too often we and our leadership step back—afraid to even acknowledge that rude behavior is creeping in. It's so much easier to look away and do nothing...and hope that whatever is threatening the confidence and calm will just disappear. It doesn't.

Wiped Out by Incivility's Force

Each morning when Jackie walked into the office, her colleagues figuratively (and some literally) held their breath. Jackie was good at what she did. With an eye for detail, she quickly detected errors and incongruities in paperwork submitted for the department's review. Jackie was like a sponge when it came to rules, regulations, and guidelines, and she was integral to the department making its numbers.

However, Jackie was also short-tempered, critical, and mercurial while engaged in her work. Condescending and blunt when asked for assistance or help, Jackie turned on the charm when it suited her. Throughout the day she pushed back her chair and rose from her desk to meander through the office. Suddenly with all the time in *her* world, Jackie stopped at colleagues' desks, with a conspiratorial smile interrupted them, and initiated conversations that quickly transitioned into office gossip. It was a regular habit for her to offer her opinion on everything she *knew* that management was doing wrong.

Jackie's behavior left her colleagues walking on eggshells. They felt they needed her knowledge and experience; her colleagues knew that management condoned her rotten behavior because she produced. They approached her with questions only as necessary; they endured her interruptions so as not to rock the boat. And they wondered why management did nothing.

The company and its leadership's tolerance of Jackie's incivility stabbed deeply at productivity. Although some of Jackie's colleagues were angry, others were hurt. Nearly all failed to produce to their potential due to Jackie's interruptions and the effect her behavior had on their ability to follow through positively, consistently, and confidently. The force of incivility ran rampant because leadership didn't demand that the uncivil behavior become civil. Perhaps if leadership had begun to understand that it's not only feelings that take hold and spread, but behaviors as well, they might have put the brakes on Jackie's disrespectful and uncivil behavior.

It's not just negative feelings that can contaminate a team when incivility occurs; bad behaviors are contagious within teams too. Incivility within a team can cause norms to shift quickly as teammates mimic one another's actions. Professors Sandra Robinson (of the University of British Columbia) and Anne O'Leary-Kelly (of the University of Arkansas) tracked 35 teams in 20 organizations and found that if employees behaved negatively—said something hurtful, started an argument, criticized or griped with coworkers, said rude things about their boss or the organization, deliberately bent or broke a company rule, damaged company property, did something that harmed the organization or boss, or did work badly, incorrectly, or slowly on purpose—their teammates were much more likely to do the same. In fact the closer the team, the more likely members were to pick up on another's bad behaviors and negative moods, including incivility.[2]

MAKING A DIFFERENCE IN THE WORLD

You and I want to make a difference, and we want that difference to be positive and beneficial to humankind. In fact, researchers tell us that one of the greatest motivators for working today is no longer the paycheck, but rather our ability to change lives for the better.[3]

So if today we think it's our duty, our obligation, our mission to bring joy, better health, and a more positive lifestyle to others, why the heck do we treat each other so miserably in the workplace? Seriously, what's going on that we want to join a cause to help another precious human being, but we don't take the time or make the effort to help our colleague, our customer, our manager, or our direct report?

Too often, we look to make a difference *out there*. We want to help the less fortunate in another community, the suffering in another demographic, the poor in another country. Yet we squander a magnificent opportunity right where we are. You and I have no idea what those around us are truly experiencing and perhaps suffering in their own lives. You and

I can make a difference right where we are! We don't always need to raise funds, create a campaign, or develop a strategic plan for someone beyond our view. We just need to nurture our relationships with other human beings right in our line of vision.

You and I have a profound influence on that person sitting right next to us, whether or not we are even aware of it. One of today's most startling statistics is the soaring rate of depression, an illness that many keep to themselves and hidden from others. According to the World Health Organization, depression currently ranks as the fourth greatest cause of human suffering and disability in the world.[4]

The colleague sitting right next to you may wear a smile, and yet may be suffering from depression. Even without our being aware of their anguish, we can mitigate their pain. You and I can affect one another in a healthful and supportive manner. According to Dr. Michael Yapko, the author of *Depression Is Contagious:*

> What we do to each other can too easily become the source of great hurt in our lives and can result in an enduring way of thinking, feeling, and relating to others. But, we are relearning something of vital importance that has been too often overlooked in recent years: Just as people can be a source of pain, they can also be a source of comfort and happiness and a way out of pain.... science is confirming what we have probably always known in our hearts: *We are built to be in positive, meaningful relationships with others in order to feel good.*[5]

You and I have this magnificent power to affect another person's life for the better. Perhaps we can start with that person sitting in the same department with us. That's how to Unleash Civility.

EXERCISE THE POWER TO INFLUENCE OTHERS

We know civility is a force that affects everyone in its path. We also know that each of us has the power to take advantage of this force. The problem is that, increasingly, we're not sure how to exercise that power. Understanding the steps we can take can launch us on the path of exercising civility. Consider some of the following actions you can take the next time you encounter incivility:

- **Be an influencer.** You have the power to influence! Whether you're a leader or not, in management, or a veteran employee, someone is picking up cues from you. If you doubt me, yawn! Soon, everyone around you will be yawning, too. But you can do better than yawn. Be positive. If your office is full of negativity, stop its flow! Whether it's office gossip or the non-stop negative reactions to management's next strategy, don't be the vehicle that keeps driving negativity.

- **Persuade naysayers.** Don't fuel the negativity of naysayers by agreeing with their "will-never-work" comments. Arguing endlessly with them won't help either. Instead, you may *quickly* point out to them that you see the situation differently.

- **Have a sense of humor.** G. K. Chesterton said, "Angels can fly because they can take themselves lightly."[6] In this age of our taking ourselves so seriously, lighten up! Don't take everything as an insult, slight, or offense.

- **Be accountable.** If you make a mistake, own up to it. When you're willing to say you blew it, others will step up to the plate of accountability as well. Trust will build.

- **Get excited about a civility culture.** How can you *not* be excited? You get to work in either a culture based on civility or a culture rooted in incivility. Once you make the commitment to a civil culture, get energized. Others will see your enthusiasm, your follow-through on your commitment, and they'll feel safe—or at least safer—to do the same.

- **Change your perspective.** Make it a game. Challenge yourself to find what's positive in any given situation. Make a list—even if you have to stretch—of three positive outcomes for any issue. An outcome might even be absurd. That's okay. You'll probably start laughing! Watch what that does to your work environment.

- **Gain momentum.** You're either moving forward, in neutral, or in reverse. Don't buy into excuses to slow down progress. Team up with a colleague to use mutual-motivation to usher in civility.

- **Forgive.** When you have the ability to read another person's mind and heart, then you may have an excuse not to forgive. Until then, forgive. You will never know why someone did what they did. Wouldn't you want forgiveness if it were offered to you?

- **Keep spirits up.** Smile. It releases endorphins and melatonin and will trick your body into feeling better. Another bonus: smiling makes you look younger! If looking like you just ditched a few years isn't important to Millennial readers, consider getting into practice. In a few years you'll be glad you did!

- **Keep calm.** Practice staying calm, and you will become increasingly slow to rile in stressful circumstances. Remember when Mom suggested counting to 10? Your calmness will rub off on others, and rather than making a stressful situation worse, you'll begin to cool down its fury.

- **Encourage personal civility.** Make civility *your* priority. Be a role model for civility, and react with civility toward others, especially when they're uncivil. (We'll talk in the next section about times when civility is *not the appropriate response.* Surprised you on that one, didn't I?)

Civility's force gives you power no matter your role, position, age, or experience. You can read about civility, you can say it's a value, but until you engage with civility, you are not taking advantage of its power. If you are not yet convinced that civility is a force that you want to empower, there's a good chance that you may be empowering another force...incivility!

THE TIME FOR INCIVILITY

There is no doubt that civility reframes relationships from toxic to trusting; however, there are times that civility is our next, not our first, step.

Say, for example, your young child runs out into the street and heads in the direction of oncoming traffic. Civility is the last thing on your mind! You grab your child, stop her from heading anywhere, and get her to safety. *Then* once calm, safe, and secure, you can begin to teach her about the dangers of playing near traffic, but in those first moments, there's no thought of courtesy, politeness, or feelings. It's a matter of safety at that moment. You did what was necessary to grab your little one's attention and bring an unsafe situation to an abrupt end.

Sometimes with adults, we need to make civility our second choice in order to grab control and bring a dicey confrontation to a grinding halt. In the throes of an emotional outburst, an employee may be so overwhelmed by his feelings that polite reasoning falls on deaf ears. Like the child running into a dangerous street, we must grab his attention. Acting as that person's mirror, we may need to reflect back to him his own behavior. That means increasing your physical, verbal, and emotional presence. How do you that? Carefully and for a very short period. If you're sitting, remain seated. Sometimes standing up encourages the misbehaver to engage in more broad and stressed gesturing. If you're already standing, be sure that your posture is erect and steady—evoking seriousness. If the person is yelling, you may need to *quickly and momentarily* raise your volume—remember, you're trying to grab his attention. If you've succeeded in wrestling their focus back to you, then you can begin to lower your volume. Your emotional presence will be communicated through your body language: Don't smile, don't sway back and forth, don't fling your arms around. Your goal is to evoke composure and confidence and a no-nonsense reaction to his obnoxious behavior. This sets the stage for civility to enter the scene.

Remember, your goal is to demonstrate respect for the other individual. When a colleague, customer, or leader is triggered so that emotions take control, that individual has become the slave to a brain on survival, not reasoning, mode. You may not respect that person's behavior at the moment, but your goal is to respect him as a fellow human being. You are attempting to transform your toxic workplace back to trusting. Ultimately, that can be achieved only through incorporating civility.

It's a very rare occurrence when civility is step two, but there are those instances when you must use momentary incivility to get to civility. Again, this should be a very rare circumstance.

Now that we have a solid understanding of how civility equals the playing field in any given situation, and before we move on to what a civil business looks like in Part II, please take a moment to review this chapter with the **Civility Wrap-up** and then **C's the Day**!

Civility Wrap-Up

- Our greatness lies in our ability to remake ourselves.

- Civility and incivility are both forces. They each affect the feelings and behaviors of others. Civility is the positive force; incivility is the negative and destructive force.

- You are a source of comfort or pain to others.

- In only the rarest of circumstances, acting with incivility paves the way to acting civilly.

C's the Day

Please revisit the section above on the many different ways you can exercise your civility for the benefit of others. Write down three things that you could do differently every day to make your workplace better for those with whom you work. Will these changes be a stretch for you? How do you think your colleagues will react to your positive changes?

Communicating Character by Exercising Civility

NOTES CHAPTER 4

1 Merriam-Webster's Collegiate Dictionary, 11th ed., s.v. "force."

2 Christine Pearson and Christine Porath, *The Cost of Bad Behavior: How Incivility Is Damaging Your Business and What to Do about It* (New York: Portfolio, 2009), 87.

3 Geoffrey James, "The Deepest Source of Motivation," Inc.com, http://www.inc.com/geoffrey-james/the-deepest-source-of-motivation.html.

4 Michael D. Yapko, *Depression Is Contagious: How the Most Common Mood Disorder Is Spreading around the World and How to Stop It* (New York: Free Press, 2009), xiii.

5 Ibid., xiv.

6 G.K. Chesterson, *Orthodoxy* (1908).

PART II: THE CIVIL BUSINESS

CHAPTER 5
Foundation of Civility: Politeness, Respect, and Trust

Why do you frequent a certain business? Sure, it provides a product that you need, like, or even love. But I'm guessing there's something more to your decision. You choose to give that business your hard-earned money because you genuinely *like* them. Spending time with that business is like spending time with a friend. There's warmth, a mutual respect, and a feeling that you can ask any question—even if it seems silly. You leave its presence with a smile on your face and a feeling that all is well with that relationship.

That's exactly how I feel when I spend time in one of my favorite shops. It deals with very high-end products and a very wealthy clientele. Businesses like this are renown for the ability to schmooze and placate their customers. Unfortunately, these companies also often have the reputation for treating their would-be customers who aren't forking over their platinum cards with condescension, if not downright rudeness. Not this dear shop. I typically spend less than $50 with them, and it's usually for some silly service. I ask questions that I probably should know the answers to, and I take up chunks of their time. They treat me with politeness, respect, and trust. In other words, they treat me with civility. They are a civil business.

Lest you think only small businesses can achieve civility, I know a gentleman who has the same feelings of delight and trust when he gets off the phone with Hewlett-Packard—a mammoth organization of more than 300 thousand employees. He's not exactly one of their big-time clients. He owns one home printer.

No matter the size, no matter the product, every business has the opportunity to be civil. It's in that organization's best interest to be a civil business not only because of the effect that civility has on its bottom line, but because of the effect civility has on us as human beings.

> *No matter the size, no matter the product, every business has the opportunity to be civil.*

Although every business has the opportunity to hit the mark of a civil business, not every business has the ability (knowledge) or willingness to do so. You deserve the opportunity to lead a civil business, to work for a civil business, and to have a fabulous relationship with a civil business.

Please join me and let me help you in your endeavor to be the civil business that you can be.

C'S THE OPPORTUNITY

Have you ever been tempted to come up with an excuse for some personal character flaw? Of course—we all have! "If my mother had only..." "If my friends just understood..." "If my spouse were a better provider..." "If only I didn't have my grandmother's temper..." "If only social media didn't reach out and grab me..." (You know you've blamed your friends' postings for robbing you of hours of precious time!)

The "if only" list could go on indefinitely. No matter how short or how long the list, our "if onlys" are just an excuse for our poor behavior, our unwillingness to confront a shortcoming, or our failure to take responsibility. I know it sounds harsh, but civility doesn't show up without attention and effort.

The 3 C's approach spells out what's at stake—you! Your character—who you truly are—is what you risk by not confronting incivility and replacing it with civility. Remember, **you *Communicate* your *Character* by how you exercise your *Civility*.** Your civility not only informs others as to who you are, civility is the vehicle to strengthen your character.

It's no different for business. The character of your business—what your organization truly stands for—is demonstrated by civility. But businesses are loaded with their own "if only" excuses. "If only corporate would provide more money..." "If only I didn't have to deal with these Millennials..." "If only I didn't have to work with these Baby Boomers..." "If only my customers were nicer..." "If only my manager wasn't such an idiot..." The fact is that civility is the result of a full contact effort by each and every one of us. Civility demands that we confront and work to eradicate incivility. Some businesses take civility seriously. Others assume that if they throw out a few generalities to the employees, those employees will comprehend the message. That doesn't work! As a result, an employee's lack of civility reflects on the company's character (think *brand*).

Recently, I was departing from an international hotel chain with a reputation for outstanding customer service. As I headed toward the huge glass double doors to exit, I could see the doorman, a young man bent down looking at his desk. Each time I'd been in and out of this hotel, I'd seen this fellow in the same position, looking down, never opening the door or even acknowledging my presence. Was he rude intentionally? I don't believe so. He wasn't trained! I started chatting with him, and he couldn't have been more upbeat and thoughtful once I had his attention. (I know what you're thinking—he was not wearing ear buds.) I asked him about training. He told me that yes, employees knew they were to take care of their customers' needs and were, in fact, given the opportunity to spend company money to turn around a customer's dissatisfaction.

New employees were told to keep the clientele happy. They just weren't told how. Obviously, there was some disconnect. How does a doorman keep customers happy if he isn't aware of their entering and exiting the hotel? How does an employee show respect when he literally doesn't see or make any connection with the patrons? When I pursued the subject of training with him, my now engaged doorman said he was sure training would happen—sometime. This young man who had the opportunity, ability, and desire to be an outstanding representative of this hotel failed because of the company's failure to provide training. He had been with the company for six months, yet he'd received nothing instructive other than "It's your job to keep the customers happy."

In today's society of fast food meals, little family time at the dinner table, and the scarcity of etiquette, it's your job as a business to provide guidance, training, and modeling of civil behavior. If not, you're chancing that what your business is exercising is incivility.

POLITENESS

There's probably no greater fan of a warm smile and a courteous greeting than I. However, too often that's all some businesses have to offer—a cursory approach to courtesy. Their friendly demeanor goes no further than the checkout counter. Once they've separated you from your money, out you go!

The customer's relationship with a business frequently replicates a dating cycle. Think about going on a first date with someone whom you find really attractive. You pull out the stops to look positively sensational; you're on your best behavior. Your conversation is all about them. You laugh at their ridiculous jokes; you even agree with their politics or favorite sports teams, which you would usually despise.

Some months or years later into that same relationship, you're at the point you throw on just about anything to wear. That date you saw as only upbeat and fascinating now seems cranky and critical to you. You roll your eyes at his or her jokes. And there is now no question as to where you stand on politics and sports. In fact, you jump at the opportunity to let him or her know exactly what you think!

Although there are businesses that too often play that same dating game, there are others that understand that **The 3 C's Rule** must be a consistent value.

The 3 C's Standard

For two years, Josie had been eyeing a job as marketing director at a mid-size company in her town. She studied the business thoroughly, ran through the series of interviews without a hitch, and now she was driving to what she considered her final interview for the position. Josie had been invited to dine with the head-honchos. She'd shopped for the perfect outfit—it was somewhat conservative, but had a special flare that hinted at her eye for design.

She'd called her mom for a quick run-through of which knife, fork, or spoon to select, and where to place it once used. She double-checked the news in case a subject in the headlines might come up in conversation. She even begged her way into the last manicure of the day at her favorite salon. Nothing was going to get in the way of the success of this last interview.

At dinner everything went well. Josie felt that the conversation was polite, intelligent, even sparkling. She congratulated herself for not dropping one morsel of food in her lap. But despite all the homework, all the attention to details, the call she received the next day was that she would not be joining her company of choice as its new marketing director.

Josie, who knew that she could be impatient and even a bit thin-skinned at times, felt confident that she had treated those who were deciding her fate with respect, and interest (even if it was feigned at times). So what went wrong? *Josie's double standards.* She may have treated the company leaders politely, but Josie's behavior toward the wait staff was curt, critical, and demanding. In other words, she could turn it on, and just as easily (if not more easily), turn it off. That inconsistent behavior amounted to multiple red flags for the company's decision makers. They couldn't risk Josie picking and choosing which clients she'd show civility to. They knew teamwork would never be dependable or predictable if Josie's respect for others was undependable and unpredictable.

These decision makers knew that if Josie was part of their organization, she would represent their organization. What they'd seen by Josie's behavior was that they couldn't depend on Josie to represent their company well.

Leaders and recruiters know that all of us can be on our best behavior one moment and then quickly turn into someone unrecognizable under pressure or in different circumstances. Often, one of their tests is in a restaurant setting. Not only do they want to see the "polish" of an applicant and whether they can handle themselves in social settings, but leaders want to see how the job seeker treats other people when those other people carry no weight as to the candidate's professional future. When civility becomes inconsistent and is exercised in bits and pieces, that person's character has been shown to be lacking.

You *Communicate* your *Character* by how you exercise your *Civility*!

Early in my television career I interviewed a young woman whose popularity was soaring in Hollywood. The beauty was to star in a new television series in a genre that usually cast men in the starring roles. As she walked into the studio, she exuded warmth and fun. She was an easy interview, answering my questions quickly and often with humor. When the interview concluded and she exited the studio, the actress smiled and thanked everyone who'd been part of the process: my producer, the studio camera operators, myself, and my co-host. A short time later I spoke with our production assistant, whom I'll call Michelle, whose job was to greet our guests and make them feel at home. There was no one better than Michelle to make guests feel welcome. When I asked Michelle about our guest, she was furious and hurt. It turns out that the actress, charming to those she thought could help her look good on camera, was rude to anyone that wasn't in the studio or the director's booth. She treated our dear and talented member of the team terribly. We never invited the tarnished star back. By the way, her highly touted show wasn't around long, either.

You tell the world who you are at your very core by how you treat others— not just the people who may hire you. As Josie and the Hollywood starlet demonstrated, inconsistency as to who received their respect told others something they surely didn't intend to communicate: their character lacked substance, integrity, and trust.

No one is immune from the temptation to limit civility to those who can help us in our move up the ladder. After all, civility takes effort, often more than we're willing to give...especially if we don't think the other person can be of service to us!

MISSED OPPORTUNITIES

Some years ago when we first moved to a new town, my husband and I went shopping for a new SUV. This was the first time this Florida girl had lived in snow, and I wanted a vehicle that was big, tough, and boasted four-wheel drive. The salesman greeted us with a huge smile (that never left his face during the entire transaction), answered all of our questions, and put me behind the wheel of a spectacular looking ride. While the ink dried on my contract, he waved goodbye, still all smiles and as polite as could be. Then came my first routine maintenance check.

When I drove in to the service department, my previously overly attentive salesman happened to walk by. He not only didn't recall my name, he didn't even recognize me. He never showed me a moment of recognition, polite or otherwise, on that first maintenance check or any time I was in the dealership thereafter.

But the sales guy wasn't alone. I was there for routine maintenance over the course of a year or two. Not once did the manager of the service department greet me by my first or last name as he took my keys and put a check mark next to my name on his department's spreadsheet of appointments. I became a number instead of a valued customer.

Your Brand, Your Behavior

My experience with my errant car dealership also points out an important lesson. I missed the opportunity to provide a much needed service. Civility is a two-way activity. If we let incivility slide, we might as well stamp the behavior with our seal of approval. If we don't expose and pluck out the uncivil behavior, it takes root and spreads. It was my responsibility to make it clear to the dealership that its approach to doing business was not acceptable behavior, at least not for me. I griped about the incidents to neighbors and friends who had had similar experiences. I indulged in self-justification, blame, and gossip with the others, but I for one, never said one word to anyone at the business.

I wasn't being civil by accepting poor customer service and choosing not to engage. I took the easy way out.

My commitment to civility should have propelled me to take the step of explaining my recurring negative experiences to someone at the dealership, especially someone at the top. It was my job to politely describe what had occurred time and time again and the effect it had on my opinion of the company.

Leadership could have then chosen to take the reins and demand a change, which in turn would have laid the groundwork for a civil business.

Have you ever been in a similar situation—on either end? As an employee, how could you improve on your customers' experiences beyond a quick hello? As a customer, what action could you take to let management know they're running a shop that's not exactly welcoming?

Short-termed politeness in the attempt to manipulate the customer is anything but civil. It's a lot closer to deception. Civility goes much deeper than a smile and a greeting; a civil business stands firmly on respect.

RESPECT

Respect for Customers

A civil business doesn't use a firm handshake, smile, and pleasantness as manipulative devices to make a quick sale. A civil business has no room for insincerity. In fact, it's exactly that type of behavior that gives civility a bad name. When civility is not grounded in respect for the other person, respect for the benefits of the product or service, and respect for creating and maintaining a relationship, civility comes off as a fraud.

A civil business is dedicated to consistency and demonstrates respect for the customers, its employees, and its community. A civil business is committed to excellence. It provides:

- Outstanding products and services on a consistent basis
- Consistent follow-up and follow-through

- Courteous behavior on a consistent basis
- Consistent dependability
- Consistently great communication

So, the formula for achieving an ideal business is
Respect + Consistency = Civility.

Respect for the Environment

Your business environment truly is a living, breathing entity that can either suffer from toxic poisoning or grow to be healthy, nurturing, and enriching. The change, especially the downward spiral from healthy to toxic, can happen quickly. However, the solvent of civility can be equally powerful in cleaning up that muck that can build up in a toxic environment of incivility.

What makes the business environment living and breathing? *Each and every human being who is part of that environment.*

Although our businesses and organizations spend vast amounts of money, commit time, and devote effort to cleaning up our communities and global environment *out there* (think recycling efforts alone), we fail to take care of the environments in which we work, interact, and strive to produce every day. Am I saying that we shouldn't work to keep and maintain a healthy environment for our world? Absolutely not! What I am saying is that there is a precious human being (even if they don't seem so precious) right in front of us that you and I affect moment by moment with what we say, how we relate, or whether or not we commit to one another and to the business.

We never truly know what takes place in another's life—the private nightmares that he never shares, the financial struggles that she battles quietly, the sleepless nights that he endures. There is no television commercial illustrating their plight or a famous movie star imploring us to help that person in front of us. There is no corporate campaign within the business to donate funds, time, or materials. There is only you and I and our ability to give of our own humanity expressed through our civility toward one another—our ongoing expression of respect for another.

Our behavior never stands alone. Our behavior punctuates our words, and our behavior takes on a life of its own, reaching out and touching those in our professional lives and in our personal lives. When was the last time you had a lousy day at work and then found yourself being short with your spouse or kids when you got home? You see, bad behavior flows downstream just as much as "pay it forward" improves the mood of the giver and the receiver. What we say really does have an effect on those around us, so choose your words carefully, especially if you're surrounded by toxicity and unpleasantness. What will you choose the next time you're in a less-than-perfect environment?

One of the most exciting results I see in my coaching is watching an environment transform from toxic to trusting by that growing awareness, accountability, and commitment to affect the lives of others in a positive way. (By the way, the result is increased effectiveness, productivity... and yes, a healthier bottom line.)

Sometimes toxicity isn't overt. You can't see it—but you can feel it! There's a chance you've experienced the heaviness of frustration, exasperation, patience that's worn thin, and communication that is sporadic and ineffective. I'm often the last-ditch effort for a business that has just about given up on an individual, who through ignorance or intention, doesn't include civility in the way he or she conducts business. The person is a fount of chaos, and as a result, colleagues and leadership are at wit's end. It's not unusual for me to hear "I'll be shocked if you can turn them around." My coaching allows me to push, prod, and help navigate an individual toward understanding the value of civility and then exhibiting it. In other words, there is a turn around and that means that everyone is moving in the same direction—toward the same goal of civility. People breathe more deeply, communication flows both ways, tension evaporates, and the toxic becomes trusting.

CIVIL LEADERSHIP IN ACTION

Most of us want to work in a civil workplace, and most leaders actually want to provide one that's civil. The problem is that often the bosses are out of touch with what's happening beyond the C-Suite. As a result, their arms-length approach to the employees leads to distrust.

Employees figure the head honchos are making big bucks and couldn't care less about the daily grind and ongoing demands of the rank and file. (Too often, that *is* the case.) Even without intentional disregard for employees, leadership's failure to engage and communicate with the men and women it leads creates the perfect environment for toxicity to germinate.

However, there are many leaders who want to establish and maintain a trusting workplace, they just don't know how. In Part III, I'll describe what it takes to go from Leader to Civil Leader.

By demanding a civil business, we provide a better experience for those within the workplace and a greater experience for those who purchase our goods and services, and that builds trust in our business and in our brand.

Walking the Talk

When Betty Garrett talks about civility, two words continually punctuate the conversation: *relationships* and *trust*. As president and CEO of one of the world's most successful speakers bureaus, Garrett Speakers International, Inc., it's Garrett's job to provide the perfect speaker with the perfect message to grace the stages of events that attract hundreds or even thousands of attendees. It's a business fraught with stress, deadlines, multiple and changing demands, audiences in front of the curtain, assistants (and often chaos) behind the curtain, and egos. The potential for incivility to erupt is enormous, but not on Garrett's watch.

For four decades Garrett has worked rigorously to build relationships and develop an enviable and rock solid reputation for stellar performance, follow-through, and trust. If she tells you she's going to provide a service, she provides it, and then goes beyond.

The speakers that she represents, many of whom command five-figure fees for an hour's speech, know exactly where Garrett stands on civility. She spells it out up front. It's not enough to be an exceptional performer; you must be a civil human being.

Walking the Talk (continued)

In Garrett's words, "I need you to be the total package. My reputation is at stake, and if you're not up to my standards and how I want you to behave onsite and to people behind the scenes, then I can't trust you. And if I can't trust you, we can't work together."

In the language of **The 3 C's**, it sounds like this: "You (speakers) Communicate my Character (my reputation and that of my business) by how you exercise your Civility (how you treat the audience *and* every person behind the curtain).

In 40 years, Garrett has had two speakers let their egos get in the way of civility. They were rude to people behind the scenes, and she did not give them a second chance. As Garrett explains, "They have to be nice to those people off stage as well as the people they face in the audience when they're on stage. If they're not nice and easy to work with, guess what, I won't hire them again. I've worked too hard to earn the respect and trust from the people I work with."

Only *two* people in 40 years didn't live up to Garrett's standards of civility. That doesn't just happen. Betty Garrett makes accountability an important part of civility. "Be perfectly clear with what you'll accept and what you won't tolerate. There can be conflict, because someone misinterpreted or miscommunicated. In dealing with people, there will always be conflict. But you still respect that person. Work on compromising. However, you never compromise on reputation!"

Civility is not only a way of doing business for Betty Garrett. It's a way of life.

TRUST

Civility isn't reserved just for customers. It's not to be spent only on the highest performers. It's not a gift to be rewarded on occasion.

Civility is a way of doing business inside and outside every organization. For any company to be truly civil, there must be respect for every individual who serves that company as an employee, and respect for every individual who supports that company as a customer.

Our society and our communities reflect the strength of our families. When our families are happy and healthy and able to cope with their struggles effectively, our communities reflect that happiness and health, and are stronger as a whole to address communal challenges. When our families are suffering from poverty, illness, and violence, the community reflects that anguish.

So it is with our businesses. What happens with a business, with its customers, and how its brand is regarded in communities reflects what is happening within the business itself. Remember that old saying, "The clothes make the man"? The outward appearance is a reflection of what's happening on the inside. What would you think if you were to walk into a clothing store that looked like a disorganized closet with garments strewn everywhere and apathetic employees? What would you think is happening in the home office? Conversely, if you were to enter a pristine clothing store that was tidy and had friendly and dedicated employees, would you think that company had its act together?

A civil business makes civility a core value in its internal relationships with employees, its external relationships with its clients, and its ongoing relationship with its community.

Civility and trust are interdependent. No trust equals no civility; no civility equals no trust. A civil business requires a foundation of trust. Civility grows from that foundation of trust, and civility leads to a foundation of trust. If you get the foundation of trust wrong, any slight tremor or any slight storm will shake the business and weaken the structure, if not see it totally collapse.

Tennis champion Arthur Ashe once said, "Trust has to be earned, and should only come after the passage of time."[1] Too often decision makers think that a clever tagline, a mandate, or an ad campaign replaces the essential ingredient of trust. Paying for a marketing campaign that excites customers outside the business as well as the employees within the company may have short-term results, but it will never withstand the test of time. Trust is earned, and it takes ongoing work! There's no shortcut to a foundation of trust and there's no quick fix when trust is compromised.

Bricks Not Bungaroosh

Beginning in the mid-eighteenth century, Brighton, England, grew from a tiny fishing village to a large town. As the town grew quickly, more buildings became necessary and were constructed using a building material called *bungaroosh*. Bungaroosh was building composite made from a mishmash of bricks (some broken), cobblestones, flints, sand, and pieces of wood. Although a popular remedy to the need for more structures in town, in the long term, bungaroosh wasn't the best permanent solution. It didn't resist water well at all. A local saying is that much of Brighton "could be demolished with a well-aimed hose."[2]

So, first things first. Take a look to see whether your foundation is strong and built on trust or whether there may be bungaroosh in it that could be the source for some concern.

But before turning the page, please take a moment to double-check the **Civility Wrap-up** and then be sure to **C's the Day!**

Civility Wrap-Up

- Civility goes further than politeness.
- Civility is *not* about manipulation or deception.
- Respect + Consistency = Civility
- Civil businesses are built on a foundation of trust.
- Transforming your environment from toxic to trusting begins with you!

C's the Day

Take a look at the next set of statements about the foundational makeup of your business and rank them from Very Poor (1) to Excellent (5).

1 = Very Poor   3 = Average, Needs Improvement   5 = Excellent

My organization is built on a strong foundation of trust.	1	2	3	4	5
My colleagues and I handle change well.	1	2	3	4	5
Leadership provides clarity as to our direction.	1	2	3	4	5
I have confidence that the environment will remain healthy during times of increased pressure and change.	1	2	3	4	5
There's a consistency I can depend on in this organization.	1	2	3	4	5
My team feels valued.	1	2	3	4	5
I feel valued and appreciated.	1	2	3	4	5
I treat my colleagues and customers with respect.	1	2	3	4	5
I take responsibility for my behavior.	1	2	3	4	5

How did you do? Do you think that your colleagues, leadership, direct reports, and customers would agree with your assessment? Read and grade each sentence with them in mind and see if the numbers match. If not, determine the gaps.

Communicating Character by Exercising Civility

NOTES CHAPTER 5

1   Arthur Ashe, BrainyQuote.com, Xplore Inc. (2015), www.brainyquote.com/quotes/
    quotes/a/arthurashe371538.html.

2   Bungaroosh, https://en.wikipedia.org/wiki/Bungaroosh.

CHAPTER 6
Obstacles to Civility

Imagine for a moment working in a civil business environment. Now imagine the effect that environment would have on you.

Would you start your day differently if you could depend on being treated respectfully at work? Rather than dragging yourself out of bed and dreading the next eight hours with your co-workers, would you look forward to the time together if you could count on not being undermined? If you knew that you could throw out your ideas without fear of ridicule or someone's condescending remark, would it make a difference? If you knew that the moment you left the room you wouldn't be the subject of gossip, would you finally feel that you could take a deep breath? If you knew that you could trust that everyone on your team would pull their own weight, would you feel less anxious (and even less resentful)? If you knew that you could get a response to your questions in a timely manner, would it allow you to move forward more quickly and with more confidence? What difference would it make in your commitment if you could depend on your leadership to model your organization's expected behavior? How would you describe your attitude if you knew that each person in your organization would hold one another accountable?

Unfortunately, too many of today's organizations are riddled with distrust, fear, lack of commitment, frustration, and wasted, unproductive hours.

Eighteenth century writer Samuel Johnson wrote that, "When once the forms of civility are violated, there remains little hope of return to kindness or decency."[1] It's more than 200 years later, and Johnson's words still perfectly describe how violating civility continues to lead to a complete collapse of kindness and even decent behavior among employees and their leaders.

One of the most truly negative byproducts of our uncivil workplace is the apathy and near despair that employees feel. If you think that my word choice of "despair" is too dramatic, you should take a look at the faces I see and hear the voices of the people who describe to me the helplessness they feel in an environment that drags them down constantly. Bosses stand by and do nothing about unchecked undermining, abusive conduct, and the wanton disregard of ethical behavior. Or worse still, the bosses are the sources of the undermining, abusive conduct.

If our goal is civility within the business, what are the obstacles that get in the way of obtaining that goal?

It's not always the obvious that deters civility. Granted, we understand that an obnoxious boss, a snippy young hire, and an obstinate Baby Boomer are all products and vehicles of incivility, but what are the underlying causes that set up an environment that gives rise and cultivates civility? Here are seven areas that businesses must address to show a real commitment to civility.

- Confusion
- Inconsistency
- Lack of Training
- Wrong People
- Zero Tolerance for Conflict
- Assumptions
- Lack of Recognition

CONFUSION

Nothing invites incivility and dissension like confusion. Unfortunately, confusion can become the official language of a business quickly! No, I'm not saying that we're speaking different international languages. I'm saying we use the same words with entirely different meanings, and then we're shocked when we don't get our desired results. What I have in my mind may be completely different from what someone else has in mind when they hear the same word.

Take the word *professional*. When you tell your direct reports you expect them to be professional in the workplace, your expectation for "professional" behavior may be far different than the way your direct reports translate the word. Professional may mean:

- Showing up at the start time of the shift **OR** showing up 10 minutes *before* start time.

- Answering the phone by the third ring **OR** answering the phone... sometime.

- Greeting customers with a smile and friendly greeting **OR** making eye contact with the customer to let them know that there is a live human being who may or may not have an answer to their questions.

- Arriving at work wearing crisp, clean, and freshly ironed clothing **OR** arriving at work in clothing that resembles pajamas.

- Paying attention to personal hygiene **OR** covering up the lack of personal hygiene with a heavy dose of perfume or aftershave.

- Asking questions about an assignment in a respectful tone **OR** grunting and muttering with disgust about an assignment.

- Completing a task on or before the deadline **OR** completing the task after the deadline. (*At least it was close!*)

- Defining tasks and goals and ensuring that everyone understands his and her responsibilities **OR** spitting out directives and expecting everyone to complete them—no questions asked.

- Behaving in a highly ethical manner **OR** behaving in a manner that may be very questionable.

- Holding one another accountable **OR** holding no one accountable. (*Why bother? No one really cares!*)

When confusion reigns as to goals, strategies, and procedures, it's impossible to be on the same path. No one knows where the path is supposed to lead!

The point is **spell it out!** Don't leave any doubt as to what your expectations are. Giving birth to confusion can be intentional or accidental. If it's intentional, it's because the person calling the shots may be a control freak and wants to ensure that only they understand the entire picture, thereby guaranteeing that other people depend on them to dole out necessary information. Unfortunately, another reason for the slow drip of necessary info is that there are people in our workplaces who love a little drama. Nothing sets up drama better than when everyone on a team is working from a different script.

I've seen supervisors not only provide insufficient info, but details that morph from one day to the next. Today their instructions for answering the phone are:

1. Put a smile on your face.
2. Answer the phone by the second ring.
3. Greet the caller with, "Good morning, you've reached XYZ Company. How may I help you?"

By the end of the week the instructions go like this:

1. No comments about a smile—or any other expression—on your face.
2. Answer the phone by the fifth ring.
3. Greet the caller with, "XYZ Company."

Same task, different expectations and instructions. The result? Drama. It won't take long for employees to correct one another, complain about one another, and begin to ratchet up frustration, anger, and drama! Eliminate any potential for the drama by spelling out your expectations clearly!

Not all confusion is intentional. Sometimes it's communication that lacks the specifics. Here are a few examples:

- Details are laced with pronouns rather than proper nouns. If you missed that day in English class, pronouns are words like *he, she, it, they, them,* and *it*. They're not specific, so that sometimes people are confused as to who "he" and "she" are. Rather than telling an employee to deliver a report to *his* office so that *they* can review it *later* that afternoon, spell out that you want the employee to deliver the report to *Jaime's* office by *noon*.

- Sometimes we don't begin at the beginning when we ask someone to complete a task. We jump in at Step 3 rather than starting at Step 1. If you begin to see your listeners' eyes glaze over, stop and double-check whether you began at the starting point and are following up in sequence.

  I learned this lesson the hard way. A friend of mine finally had had enough of my kicking off a story midway as she tried frantically to figure out all the missing pieces. She was frustrated, and actually felt stupid that she couldn't follow me. Midsentence she stopped me, and very emphatically let me know that I always start in the middle of a story. Why had I gotten into that habit? I thought I was doing my listeners a favor. I didn't want to waste their time with too many details.

- Sometimes we assume the person learns the way we do. I'm a visual and aural learner. Sorry, you have to tell me, and then show me those visuals, too! My husband, on the other hand, dives right in and learns experientially. My way of learning is redundant for my husband; his way of learning would be less effective for me. If people aren't learning their tasks because instructional styles don't align with learning needs, they and those with whom they work can become frustrated, and frustration can quickly launch into incivility.

INCONSISTENCY

The kissing cousin to confusion is inconsistency. Perhaps, you've experienced some of these examples of inconsistent standards or expectations:

- Everyone is expected to show up at work at a specific time except for a few members of the "in" crowd.
- The work results are inconsistent: excellent one day, mediocre the next.
- The expectations by management for work results are inconsistent: What is considered outstanding work one week is considered sub-par the next week.

- Moods flip quickly, and everyone treads lightly trying to read "happy" or "angry."
- Office gossip is grounds for disciplinary action one day. Later in the month it's nearly encouraged.
- Dress codes are inconsistently applied. Employees at one department store told me that everyone was held to a fairly conservative dress code (for women, think hems that strike the knee, high necklines, and closed toe shoes; for men, ties are required). However, when one young woman wore plunging necklines and short skirts, there were no repercussions. Other women had been sent home to change for the same unacceptable clothing.

Inconsistent behavior and standards lead to frustration, doubt, and anger. Civility doesn't have a chance to take root when people are frustrated—what's acceptable one day isn't the next. When people are in doubt, they can't focus. Tasks take longer, are less creative, and are of lower quality. Angry outbursts and angry silence quickly become part of the culture.

LACK OF TRAINING

Like confusion and inconsistency, when people are in the dark as to how to do their job, what the expected standards are, and what defines acceptable behavior, people are at odds rather than together as a team. Lack of training is a perfect way to extend an invitation to incivility. Businesses set up the perfect conditions for incivility when they don't provide adequate training.

Employees require training to understand:

- The skills necessary to do the job
- The expectations for that job
- The behavior that is acceptable for a civil business with the public as well as with one another
- How to argue and still maintain civility

Training Skills

One of the most disrespectful actions businesses can take is to set up employees—at any level—for failure by not providing adequate training. I know, I know—there's no money, there's no time, there's no way to train. There is, however, creativity. Show enough respect for your employees to come up with alternatives to expensive training that can still help prepare the individual to do their job and meet expected standards. In many communities, local colleges provide free or low-cost training on various subjects that can help someone in their new position. Assigning a mentor can help smooth the way. Realize that every responsibility has a soft skills side as well as the hard skills piece. Provide a resource library of books—including this one!—CDs, DVDs, and online training that employees can use for referral and their own clarification.

Clear Expectations

Civil companies don't make employees guess as to what the final product should look like. For example, it's clear that what's acceptable behavior for online customer service at one company is intolerable at another. Remember the gentleman I mentioned who buys printers only from Hewlett-Packard? He's loyal because no matter what customer service rep he deals with, my friend is treated kindly. When he asks a question, the response is respectful and often accompanied with humor—but not at his expense! His background has little to do with technology, so his questions are basic and fundamental, yet there's not the slightest hint of condescension from the HP employee. Every time he calls with a question, he always hangs up the phone and declares, "I will never buy a printer from anyone but HP." My friend often calls HP, which means that he's constantly dealing with different customer reps. Different people, but always the same excellent service. Obviously, HP's employees all know what the expected experience for an HP customer should sound like and look like.

Model Desired Behavior

Civil companies not only make it clear what acceptable behavior is, they model that behavior. The Irish writer and poet Oliver Goldsmith said, "People seldom improve when they have no other model but themselves to copy after."[2]

When the newcomer walks into the business and hears peers gossiping about one another, listens to team members responding to questions with sarcasm and a surly attitude, and sees that management doesn't engage, that newcomer finds no one modeling the positive and desired behavior. As Goldsmith says, they're stuck with no model for improvement.

How to Argue with Civility

Civility does not mean people don't argue. You'll never get the best of the best if people aren't free to voice their disagreement, contrasting ideas, and what they see as weaknesses and errors. But *how* to argue and maintain respect is a skill that must be taught, modeled, and mentored.

Fear of confrontation and a walking-on-eggshells attitude are the enemies of a company that wants the best for its customers and its employees.

WRONG PEOPLE

If highly qualified people who love what they do and get excited about out-of-this-world results are forced to work with folks who get by with doing the minimum work and are satisfied with substandard results, watch out! You have the makings of a company that's in trouble, a lot of bungaroosh in the mix, and it won't be long before resentment, frustration, and anger give rise to disrespect, if not downright contempt.

In Jim Collins' best seller *Good to Great*, the book one young executive friend of mine calls his bible for business, Collins quotes a Wells Fargo executive as saying, "The only way to deliver to the people who are achieving is to not burden them with the people who are not achieving."[3] At a quick glance, that may seem anything but civil because to ensure that people who achieve are surrounded by others who achieve, the non-achievers have to go. It doesn't look particularly civil when people are fired or demoted, but when, despite repeated training, encouragement, and intervention, the non-achiever can't learn the skills or change attitudes, there's only one civil step left. Show respect for those who are working to achieve excellent standards and surround them with achievers.

Collins spells this out so well in his Practical Discipline #2: When you know you need to make a people change, act.

> The moment you feel the need to tightly manage someone, you've made a hiring mistake. The best people don't need to be managed. Guided, taught, led—yes. But not tightly managed. We've all experienced or observed the following scenario. We have a wrong person on the bus and we know it. Yet we wait, we delay, we try alternatives, we give a third and fourth chance, we hope that the situation will improve, we invest time in trying to properly manage the person, we build little systems to compensate for his shortcomings, and so forth. But the situation doesn't improve. When we go home, we find our energy diverted by thinking (or talking to our spouses) about that person. Worse, all the time and energy we spend on that one person siphons energy away from developing and working with all the right people. We continue to stumble along until the person leaves on his own (to our great sense of relief) or we finally act (also to our great sense of relief). Meanwhile, our best people wonder, "What took you so long?"[4]

ZERO TOLERANCE FOR CONFLICT

Although it may seem counterintuitive, civility does not prohibit conflict. In fact, conflict can lead to a healthier environment because people get to have their say; they get the opportunity to voice their concerns, or even their opposition to some idea. What's different about conflict in a civil company is that it doesn't leave the environment toxic and weaker, but actually healthier and stronger. Again, I quote from *Good to Great:*

> Indeed, one of the crucial elements in taking a company from good to great is somewhat paradoxical. You need executives, on the one hand, who argue and debate—sometimes violently—in pursuit of the best answers, yet, on the other hand, who unify fully behind a decision, regardless of parochial interests.[5]

Conflict is not the death knell for civility. It may, in fact, be just what the civil business needs.

ASSUMPTIONS

We all know what happens when we assume; more often than not, we blow it! Yet, time after time, leader after leader tells me that they assumed the individual (who's now on the brink of losing their job) knew what to do in a particular circumstance: how to behave, how to follow-through, how to handle the situation. When I ask whether they'd told the person who's now in the hot seat what to do, the leaders respond, "I just assumed they'd know!"

If you have teenagers, you know that generalizations don't work. Telling your son (or daughter) to be home in time to get a good night's sleep for school is tantamount to saying to come home whenever the mood strikes him. If you intend to see him before dawn, you have to clearly tell him the exact time he's to walk in the front door. For added emphasis, text it to him as well! Whenever you have an expectation for some result, make it clear. Don't assume the person knows what you mean. If you're tempted to say, "I assume...," check yourself. This may be a moment to toss the assumption, and train for the specifics.

LACK OF RECOGNITION

When employees feel they're not valued, appreciated, or recognized for their efforts, they stop making the effort. They also lose respect for the business, its leadership, and often their own team.

You may agree with this statement, or you may feel that employees are supposed to just do their job without expecting anything in thanks beyond a paycheck and benefits. "They're getting paid—that's enough thanks." "They shouldn't need to be coddled." "I shouldn't have to tell them what a great job they did." I agree with the "no coddling" statement; I also agree that you don't have to constantly pat someone on the back for doing *their* job. However, appreciation for special effort, particularly high quality work, and staying calm in a stressful situation are reasons for applause. Clients tell me—with a huge smile on their faces—how valued they felt when they received an "attaboy" or "attagirl" from the boss or colleague.

My first news director was demanding, blunt, and expected excellence day in and day out. He was also one of the best, if not *the* best, bosses I ever had. He didn't hand out accolades easily. However, when my work was rewarded with his "well done," I was inspired to be even more diligent and dedicated myself to taking it to the next level no matter the effort that entailed.

Although it's popular to vilify competition, the fact is that each organization, each business, each entity is in competition with others as well as with itself. As human beings in search of excellence, we compete with ourselves. There's yesterday's self and today's self. It's an exciting and productive competition (if approached correctly) that prompts us to improve today on what we did yesterday, to build on yesterday's foundation. Appreciation often gives us a guide as to how we're doing—where we're excelling and where there's room for work.

Without the "well done," we don't have a gauge to measure our progress. Without the "thank you" we feel less valued for our contribution.

Ralph Waldo Emerson said, "Our chief want is someone who will inspire us to be what we know we could be."[6] Appreciation just may be that inspiration.

In this chapter, we've identified seven obstacles to civility. Each obstacle invites frustration, chaos, worry, and anger. So if these seven items get in the way of a civil business, what elements encourage the building and maintaining a civil business? Glad you asked. That's exactly where we're heading in the next chapter. But first, let's tackle the **Civility Wrap-up** and then **C's the Day**.

Civility Wrap-Up

- There are seven obstacles to a civil business:

  - Confusion

  - Inconsistency

  - Lack of Training

  - Wrong People

  - Zero Tolerance for Conflict

  - Assumptions

  - Lack of Recognition

- "When once the forms of civility are violated, there remains little hope of return to kindness or decency." —Samuel Johnson

- "People seldom improve when they have no other model but themselves to copy after." —Oliver Goldsmith

C's the Day

Consider the seven obstacles that get in the way of your doing your best to create or maintain a civil environment. Choose one obstacle that challenges you the most. Write it down and make a plan on how you can diminish or eradicate that obstacle from your day.

Communicating Character by Exercising Civility

NOTES CHAPTER 6

1   Samuel Johnson Sound Byte Page, www.samueljohnson.com/manners.html.

2   "Oliver Goldsmith," Bartleby.com, www.bartleby.com/349/authors/86.html.

3   Jim Collins, *Good to Great: Why Some Companies Make the Leap...and Others Don't* (New York: HarperCollins, 2011), 53.

4   Ibid., 56.

5   Ibid., 60.

6   Ralph Waldo Emerson, Values.com, www.values.com/inspirational-quotes/7075-our-chief-want-is-someone-who-will-inspire-us.

CHAPTER 7
Elements of Civility

So now that we know the behaviors and thought processes that deter and destroy a civil culture, let's look at the proactive behaviors that counter the would-be deterrents and destroyers of a civil culture. There are seven elements that are essential for your civil culture to grab hold and take root:

- Clarity
- Code of Conduct
- No Asshole Rule (Please, don't be offended by the language...I'll explain later in this chapter!)
- Model Great Behavior
- Accountability
- Civil Fighting
- Hire with Civility in Mind

CLARITY

The first time I was sent out on a story as a young, inexperienced reporter, I didn't have a clue what to do or how to do it. I'd been working as the administrative assistant to the news director during my regular hours on the job. Every spare moment, including early morning and late night hours, I was hanging out in the newsroom, watching to see how the reporters, camera operators, directors, producers, and assignment editors all came together to create this glorious piece called a "news story." I watched, I hovered, I listened...but it wasn't yet up to me to produce a product—in my case, a story. That is until one day, we had too many stories and too few reporters. I was assigned to work with a veteran cameraman, Mike, and sent out to cover a teachers' strike in Miami, Florida. When we arrived on the scene, what had seemed so clear-cut from afar was a lot more confusing now that it was my responsibility to tell the story for the 10:00 p.m. news. I looked at Mike and said, "Uh, what do I do?" Mike basically took my hand and said, "Here, take the mic and go ask him (pointing to the superintendent of schools) this question." And that's how it went for the next hour: step-by-step directions on the *whats* and *hows* of my new responsibility. Back in the newsroom, I pulled up a chair and started banging away at the typewriter (ancient predecessor to today's computer keyboard). I typed word after word and knew I'd written the perfect script for this important story of the day. It all went well until Mike took a look: "Great words, kid, but that's not what's on film. Write for the message *and* the visual."

It's hard enough to take on a new job, new task, or new duty, but when employees don't have a clear map of where they're heading, the desired destination will never be reached. Civility demands handing out roadmaps to employees, and sometimes those roadmaps come in the forms of mentors and coaches.

Clarity helps to tamp down the negative emotions of doubt and fear that can too easily result in incivility toward others! A news team may not always agree. Certainly, my camera operators and I didn't always see a story the same way or how it should be told. But my colleagues were the picture of respectful behavior—even during our heated discussions—and as a result, my experiences with them were always wonderful. Trust was at the heart of every one of our relationships.

CODE OF CONDUCT

Codes of conduct aren't created quickly in a barnburner brainstorming session. They are drawn from experience—from trial and error. Codes of conduct have a purpose—to specify the values and behaviors that a business believes will foster excellent work, trusting relationships, and that will serve as guides through stressful times.

All codes of conduct are not the same. They may have similar goals of a respectful workplace and adherence to core values, but the specifics will differ. The newsrooms I worked in and loved were filled with people who were passionate about getting the story right and being the first to get it on the air. Passion isn't always the perfect mate for civility. Passion, coupled with tight deadlines, sometimes led to shouting, demanding, criticizing, and even getting angry. But that same passion, driven by respect for one another, respect for our product, and respect for our viewers, fueled relationships that held together under extremely difficult circumstances. To the outsider, it looked like chaos; to those doing the work, it was fierce harmony.

If someone were to walk into a bank and see behavior like that of our newsroom, they'd probably head in the other direction and take their money elsewhere. The bank's code of conduct may have the same destination, but took an entirely different route to get there.

When the code of conduct is modeled throughout an organization from the top down, expectations are known and therefore can be met. Spelling out a code of conduct, and then adhering to it, makes for a foundation built on trust.

NO ASSHOLE RULE

Stanford Professor Robert Sutton sent shockwaves through the business community—as well as through all polite society—when his book *The No Asshole Rule* hit the market.[1] Even I, no fan of obscenities, was shocked to read the nasty treatment he received because of the title of the book. The fact is the book's title grabs us immediately—there's no doubt whatsoever what it's about. We've all worked with people we could only describe as assholes...or what I'll more politely refer to as jerks.

The title also adds clarity. For instance, if you've read to this point, and you're still not sure whether your company measures up as a civil company, let me ask you a question: Does your workplace tolerate jerks?

You very well may be nodding your head *vigorously*, "YES! My workplace is plagued by jerks." In fact, you may look around and run out of fingers and toes to count them. Too often, out of fear of legal reprisals, insecurities about confronting the offensive behavior, or mixed messages within the organization, jerks not only are tolerated, they abound and are even promoted. And the permeation of jerks knows no limit as to sectors. Whether you work in a small business, a large publicly held corporation, a non-profit organization, or a government agency, there's a good chance that you may have experienced your share of jerks. (There also may be a chance that you have actually been a jerk at some point. We're all guilty as charged from time to time.) Let's face it, we're not always on our best behavior, especially in a business that turns a blind eye to incivility or doesn't hold respect in the workplace as a value to be protected and promoted.

The danger in tolerating obnoxious behavior—even from our leaders and high performers—is that the germ spreads quickly. Not only do emotions spread, but behaviors spread as well. Think about how you feel working with that upbeat, fun, positive person at work who sees every obstacle as an opportunity. Now consider working with someone who hasn't smiled since her fifth grade birthday party. She *knows* that your efforts to complete the project are wasted. You're invigorated by working with Ms. Upbeat; you'd rather spend the afternoon with your mother-in-law who still doesn't remember your name than Ms. Drag-You-Down.

It turns out that we pick up not only on the emotions of others, but their behaviors as well. I've watched organizations transform from professional behavior to locking colleagues out of the office and physically walking right "through" people when rude behavior was allowed to not only enter the establishments, but permeate throughout.

As offensive and ironic as the language may be, the no asshole rule has merit when applied consistently in a civil workplace.

MODEL GREAT BEHAVIOR

We're not immune from absorbing what's around us, especially when it comes to behavior. A civil business models great behavior from the top down. It's expected from every individual in the organization, up to and including the big kahuna. If you spend any time with someone who has great posture, it's not long before you pull up your chin, throw back your head a bit, and suck in your gut! You and I emulate great behavior.

The problem is that behavior that *looks* civil may not be behavior that *is* civil. Too often we're afraid of delivering bad news. We hide poor sales, inappropriate conduct, and missed deadlines. We're tempted to use the excuse of "civility," but it's anything but civil to conceal the truth. Fear of retribution from the boss can lead to disaster, but sometimes self-preservation trumps doing the right thing.

In Hans Christian Anderson's famous fairy tale *The Emperor's New Clothes*, two unscrupulous weavers come to town to convince the emperor that—at his great expense—they will create for him a spectacular new suit of clothing. The frauds collect their money, but never sew a stitch. The duo convince the ruler that their fabric is so magnificent that only those citizens who are worthy of their positions can see the tailors' apparel. When the emperor proudly parades through town to show the townspeople his expensive and splendid new garb, everyone applauds. The only problem? The emperor is naked, yet no one is willing to speak up out of fear for their positions—including the emperor who never once could see any fabric. The only one to tell the truth was an innocent little boy. Out of fear, all but one toddler were silent. As a result the emperor appeared the fool and a failure.[2]

The Emperor's New Clothes phenomenon isn't limited to fairy tales. History tells us that millions of Chinese citizens died over several years beginning in 1958 because telling the truth was tantamount to suicide. As between 20 million and 43 million Chinese citizens died, the Communist government blamed natural disasters. (Researchers estimate that there were an additional 45 million premature deaths during this same period.) However, it turns out that Mao Zedong's drastic farm policies were primarily to blame. Most believe that the government covered up the rising death tolls.

Lu Baoguo, a Xinhua reporter in Xinyang, told Yang Jisheng of why he never reported on his experience:

> In the second half of 1959, I took a long-distance bus from Xinyang to Luoshan and Gushi. Out of the window, I saw one corpse after another in the ditches. On the bus, no one dared to mention the dead. In one county, Guangshan, one-third of the people had died.

> Although there were dead people everywhere, the local leaders enjoyed good meals and fine liquor....I had seen people who had told the truth being destroyed. Did I dare to write it?[3]

Fear and intimidation are cruel and swift methods to ensure that even the most toxic of environments prosper.

Keeping quiet when speaking out is what's needed isn't always the result of fear of the boss's response. Too often detrimental silence arises from ambivalence toward the organization or its leadership, protection of guilty parties, or fear that any possible change resulting from bringing the unwelcome news to light could affect the bearer of that news adversely.

Sometimes, however, it can also come from a misplaced sense of loyalty. We don't want to burden the leader with bad news. Surely the problem will get fixed, and *then* we'll be able to report the successful turn-around. **That rarely happens**.

To demonstrate true respect for the business and for its leadership, as well as for everyone dependent on its paycheck, it's mandatory to open the curtains to the truth...especially when it's bad. Without what Jim Collins in his book *Good to Great* calls the "brutal facts," the business is in a far weaker position: "You absolutely cannot make a series of good decisions without first confronting the brutal facts."[4]

Leaders model civil behavior by sending the clear signal that the messengers of bad news will not be punished for bringing the "brutal facts" to light. Employees model civil behavior by their willingness to come forth with the truth.

ACCOUNTABILITY

Watch little kids and you learn about accountability fast! Kids know the rules, and they're not about to let anyone get away with pushing, much less breaking, those rules. They're quick to shout out the other kid's name, tell him that the ball *did* touch him, and that he is out of the game! Granted, there may be some back-and-forth squabbling for a bit, but soon all the other kids are on board and tell the offender it's time to sit out this game. (Often the kids do a far better job of holding one another accountable *before* parents jump in!)

When everyone knows the rules and everyone agrees that they're going to play by the rules, accountability can crank into gear. We may not like it when someone we supervise points out that we're not playing by the rule book, but it's critical that we pay attention and model good behavior by showing accountability for our own actions. The manner in which we hold one another accountable is vitally important, too. If you employ embarrassment, ridicule, or name-calling, you're not holding someone accountable; you're trying to bolster yourself by shredding another individual's reputation.

When an organization's code of conduct requires both punctuality and accountability, you have every right and responsibility to confront Mr. Latecomer who consistently shows up five minutes late, laughingly ending a phone call as he walks in the door. Pulling him aside and politely pointing out that he's disrespectful of others' time as well as of breaking the code of conduct is absolutely appropriate, especially the first time you address the offender's rude behavior with him. Berating him with a sarcastic "nice of you to show up" in front of the others will succeed in humiliating him and reflecting poorly on you. Holding someone accountable doesn't include jerk behavior.

I was recently in a store to pick up an order that obviously had been placed in the incorrect holding area. The owner struggled to locate my items. A young woman—a new employee with whom I'd placed my order—was called to the counter to aid in the search. She immediately found my package and handed it to me. The owner didn't hide her displeasure with her worker for a moment, glaring at the employee in annoyance. The angry look by the proprietor, who was likely embarrassed by the delay, accompanied her under-the-breath comments about the newbie not following procedure. Although the new hire may have learned the hard way about where to place orders, it was the boss who failed to be accountable for her own public behavior toward her employee. The lesson left me, as a customer, feeling uncomfortable and sympathetic toward the new employee—and not anxious to return.

CIVIL FIGHTING

The problem with civility is that people sometimes hide behind it. Rather than confronting, arguing, standing up for what's right, they say they want to maintain "civility." Hogwash! Civility is *not* about everyone getting along. Every description of America's founding fathers includes men pounding tavern tables as they vigorously debated this country's birth. In Doris Kearns Goodwin's bestseller *Team of Rivals,* she highlights President Abraham Lincoln's brilliance in surrounding himself with his political opponents, ensuring that he would hear all sides of every issue.[5]

I'm sure that the author of *The No Asshole Rule* would applaud Lincoln's unorthodox approach. Professor Sutton, who eschews the concept of "turning your organization into a paradise for conflict-averse wimps," writes:

> The best groups and organizations—especially the most creative ones—are places where people know how to fight. At Intel, the largest semiconductor maker in the world, all full-time employees are given training in "constructive confrontation," a hallmark of the company culture. Leaders and corporate trainers emphasize that bad things happen when "the bullies win," when fighting means personal attacks, disrespect, and rude intimidation. The ill effects include "only the loudest and strongest voices get heard," "no diversity of views," poor communication, high tension, low productivity, and the belief that people are first "resigned" to living with the nastiness and then "resign" from the company.[6]

Civility invites confrontation—as long as it's respectful and is in accord with the no asshole rule.

HIRE WITH CIVILITY IN MIND

Just as recruiters put on their best face when hiring, applicants can sure come across as dream employees...just until the probation period ends. Then watch out!

It's vital that during the hiring process, expectations for the responsibilities in skills and the obligations of behavior are spelled out. By showing clearly what civil behavior looks like in the organization, applicants can back out early if they realize they won't be a good fit. One way that often helps show an applicant's real approach to working cohesively is to interview more than one applicant in a group setting. It's interesting to see what behaviors come to surface when several applicants compete for the recruiters' attention. I once sat in on a group interview in which about a dozen female applicants sat in a semicircle as several of us, as supervisors and managers, asked questions and talked through common scenarios. One applicant constantly interrupted, raised her voice, and came across as obnoxious as she vied for full attention. Her inability to work with others was immediately obvious.

Too often, a sparkling smile, easy conversation, and a resume listing appropriate skill sets is the easy way to fill the opening...only to lead to disaster down the road.

INSIDE OUT AND OUTSIDE IN

Civility has to run throughout a company. Only by building on a foundation of trust and accountability, brought to fruition through civility, can a business serve all players whether it's the customer, the employee, the leader, or the community.

Knowing which elements to avoid and which ones to incorporate maps out the way to continually and consistently attain and maintain a civil culture—one that responds to the ongoing changes and challenges in any organization.

As much as everyone may be on board with the idea of heading in the direction of civility, it's up to leadership to steer the business through some nasty waters to reach the destination. In Part III, we'll investigate the Civil Leader, but you know the drill by now. First, take a look at the **Civility Wrap-up** and then **C's the Day**.

Civility Wrap-Up

- There are seven elements to establishing a civil business:
  - Clarity
  - Code of Conduct
  - No Asshole Rule
  - Model Great Behavior
  - Accountability
  - Civil Fighting
  - Hire with Civility in Mind
- "You absolutely cannot make a series of good decisions without first confronting the brutal facts." —Jim Collins
- Civility, by incorporating the no asshole rule, does not mean "turning your organization into a paradise for conflict-averse wimps." —Robert Sutton

C's the Day

Reflect on the seven elements essential to establishing and maintaining a civil business. Choose one element that you can begin to incorporate in your civil behavior...starting now! Then set daily goals for yourself and track how you're attaining your new changes. Are you hitting your new goals? Where do you need to improve if you're not?

Communicating Character by Exercising Civility

NOTES CHAPTER 7

1 Robert Sutton, *The No Asshole Rule: Building a Civilized Workplace and Surviving One That Isn't* (New York: Business Plus, 2007), 192–3.

2 Hans Christian Anderson, *Keiserens nye Klæder* (*The Emperor's New Clothes*), trans. Jean Hersholt, 1837.

3 "Great Chinese Famine," https://en.wikipedia.org/wiki/Great_Chinese_Famine.

4 Jim Collins, *Good to Great: Why Some Companies Make the Leap…and Others Don't* (New York: HarperBusiness, 2001), 70.

5 Doris Kearns Goodwin, *Team of Rivals: The Political Genius of Abraham Lincoln* (New York: Simon & Schuster, 2006).

6 Robert Sutton, *The No Asshole Rule: Building a Civilized Workplace and Surviving One That Isn't* (New York: Business Plus, 2007), 78.

PART III: THE CIVIL LEADER

CHAPTER 8
Establishing and Maintaining Trust

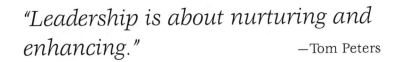 *"Leadership is about nurturing and enhancing."*
—Tom Peters

"You want me to unleash what?" you ask. Civility, dear leader, civility! The reason? Trust!

Civil leaders treasure trust. They nurture trust. Trust is the diamond that is mined, polished, and protected continually. Civil leaders are vigilant, systematic, and uncompromising about guarding this precious gem of trust, especially in today's environment that increasingly finds trust in short supply.

When the public relations firm Edelman Trust conducted its 2013 Edelman Trust Barometer, a global survey that measured trust, less than one in five respondents indicated that they believed that a business or government leader would tell the truth when confronted with a difficult issue. The Trust Barometer furthermore indicated that globally, trust in business to do what is right was at 50 percent, whereas trust in business leaders to tell the truth was 18 percent.[1] Allow me to repeat: *trust in business leaders to tell the truth was 18 percent.*

Business leaders have a horrid reputation! Imagine the fallout of a mindset that has leadership and trust at odds. Is it any wonder employees complain of toxic work environments and companies find themselves in a defensive mode with unhappy customers? Much of society, apparently, doesn't think that businesses and business leaders are particularly worthy of trust. Not exactly the making of professional relationships built on a strong foundation.

Every relationship you and I have is either built on trust or shattered by a breach of trust. It doesn't matter if it's the personal relationship of a friendship, a marriage, or that of a parent and child. Whether it's the professional relationship between a leader and his or her team, a business and its clients, or the connection between colleagues—every positive and healthy relationship depends on trust. You and I know this, and yet sometimes we don't take the steps necessary to cultivate trust, nurture that trust, and repair that trust when we have the ability to do so.

Roger Staubach, Hall of Fame quarterback and real estate entrepreneur, says that "If you don't have trust inside your company, then you can't transfer it to your customers."[2]

So it begins with what's happening *inside* the business. No trust inside the company means that there is a very real possibility that the internal lack of trust will bleed over to the lack of trust by the customers. When customers don't trust the business—goodbye business!

In a business that lacks a civil culture, distrust just seems to ooze out. I used to stop at a fast food restaurant to pick up an iced tea after dropping off my kids at school. There'd be a long line at the drive-through, so I'd quickly park and head inside. Without fail, the employees would be griping about management, schedules, or another colleague to each other within earshot of the customers. Actually, if they'd grumbled to those of us waiting to be served, they may have noticed our looks of hunger and thirst more quickly. However, more often than not, they were slow to take orders, so immersed were they in their grousing. When these young employees did disengage from the gossip huddle

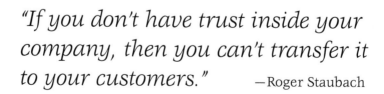

"If you don't have trust inside your company, then you can't transfer it to your customers." —Roger Staubach

to find that paying customers were waiting to place their orders, they approached us as if we were an inconvenience. Throughout the entire time I waited my turn to place my order, pay my money, and pick up my empty beverage cup for self-serve, the boss-bashing continued. No matter what morning, no matter what set of employees, the chatter was the same. Complaints about managers, schedules, and their crummy jobs composed the elevator music at the counter. All that negativity was *not* the way I wanted to start my day, and I took my business elsewhere. You may be thinking, "all that establishment lost with my heading down the street was a buck or two," and you'd be correct. However, the loss of all business begins with one customer's departure.

The environment of the fast food franchise was toxic! Leadership may have trained on how to coordinate timing of the kitchen with the counter and the takeout windows, but management failed to lay down the specifics of how to set up and maintain an environment that leads to confidence and satisfaction by its customers. As a customer, I couldn't trust that I'd receive service in a timely or polite manner, and that left me with a bad taste!

Although my experience in *this* particular restaurant was with a younger generation, negativity does not age discriminate. I've heard my share of negativity from employees working with the public who could be the parents or grandparents of our Millennials.

You may excuse their negativity because theirs was a minimum wage job. Yet I've been in plenty of coffee shops and fast food franchises where the employees serving the public don't engage in the negative chatter. They're all about smiles and service.

Exhaustion as the culprit? Of course it could be, especially because many people of all ages take a minimum wage job to supplement other income and are working far more than a 40-hour week. Less sleep, increased stress, an economy that rewards some sectors while punishing others are all contributors to an uncivil or toxic environment. But the civil leader works with these individuals so that they don't take it out on their customers or one another.

The trust inside your company begins with you, its leader. It's up to you: Demand a culture of civility. Promote the culture of civility. Model the culture of civility.

WHO MODELS WHAT?

One of the greatest sources of incivility, disrespectful behavior, and rudeness in the workplace is confusion. Like kids whose parents have totally different parenting styles—one very lenient, and one very disciplined—employees begin to take advantage of the mixed messaging, sometimes intentionally, sometimes because bad habits have become the norm.

The combination of civility and leadership has unsurpassed value in the workplace, and when *you* combine civility with your leadership, *you* have unsurpassed value. To lead with civility is to set up a foundation for trust, and a safe emotional environment that invites positive change, progress, and success. In contrast, to lead without civility and trust is to invite confusion, distrust, drama, chaos, fear, and negativity into the workplace—all which lead to increased costs and losses that can spell the end of your business.

When you combine civility with your leadership, you have unsurpassed value.

YOU SAY YOU'RE NOT A LEADER?

This chapter is every bit as important for those of you who have not yet stepped into the role of manager, boss, supervisor, director—in other words, a position of authority over other people! Don't skip Part III just because you or someone else hasn't yet identified you as a leader.

You may not have a title on a door—heck, you may not even have an office with a door! You may not have some official designation on your business card (if you even have a business card), but that doesn't mean you don't have what it takes to be a leader. This chapter is meant for everyone who is a leader now, or has any yearning to be in leadership in the future. That means this is for *you!*

As leadership expert John Maxwell says, "Leadership is not about titles, positions, or flowcharts. It is about one life influencing another."[3] No matter your title, role, responsibility, or position, you *are* influencing others right now. My question to you is this: *How* are you influencing those around you?

- Does your influence leave that other person in a better state of mind to do their job...or worse?
- Does your influence lead to teamwork that doesn't include drama or are you in the starring role?
- Does your influence lead to trust or distrust?
- Does your influence foster engagement or drain the folks you lead?
- Does your influence have the underpinnings of civility?

CIVILITY: TOP-DOWN, BOTTOM-UP

One of my favorite stories about influence comes from Linda Kaplan Thaler and Robin Koval's book, *The Power of Nice.* At the time the described incident took place, these women—two giants in the world of advertising—were CEO and president, respectively, of The Kaplan Thaler Group. In *The Power of Nice* they describe the influence that one security guard at their Manhattan office building had on not only the men and women entering and exiting the building, but on their business itself. The authors describe Frank as a large, jovial security guard in his mid-fifties who worked magic. Single handedly, Frank transformed mornings from blah to bright and upbeat. The man at the building's entrance changed the look and feel of each morning. Frank greeted people by their names and wished them a great day. In Kaplan Thaler and Koval's words:

> Frank's engaging banter changed the way we started work in the morning. Instead of simply flashing our passes anonymously and making a beeline for the elevator, we found ourselves seeking out Frank and making sure to say hello. He set a positive tone for the entire day. But we never considered how Frank might be helping our business, other than preventing intruders from entering the premises.[4]

Did you notice that Frank's effect was so positive that people took the time to search him out first thing in the morning? Frank influenced the environment—that upbeat attitude rubbed off on others and, it turned out, influenced business.

While Frank was opening doors and greeting people with his infectious smile, the two owners of the ad agency and their team were busy trying to land the account of U.S. Bank, the sixth-largest bank in the United States. It was down to the wire and their agency was competing against one last contender. Richard Davis, the president and COO of U.S. Bank, and his team would now head to the New York offices of Kaplan Thaler, evaluate the agency, meet the team, and hear its final pitch. The only problem? The bank president and his people were not keen on a trip to New York City. The bank's executive offices are in Minneapolis; spending time in the Big Apple with its reputation for abrasiveness and indifference was not appealing. However, as the authors describe, when Davis and his team showed up, opinions reversed quickly.

> ...when Richard Davis and his team walked into our building, they received a warm, enthusiastic greeting from Frank. When Davis reached our offices a few minutes later he was gushing about the friendly security guard. "This guy gave me a huge hello!" he said. "And all of a sudden, I thought how could I *not* want to work with a company that has someone like Frank? How can I feel anything but good about hiring an agency like that?" We won the account.[5]

Obviously, the ad agency didn't win the account solely because of Frank's influence, but his positive effect certainly rolled out the red carpet. The agency performed, but Frank paved the way by touching the hearts of Richard Davis and his team. Frank showed that civility is, indeed, a force that touches everyone and can be genuinely exercised by every member of an organization, whether they're the CEO or buoyant doorman!

My goal in the next few chapters is for you to begin to appreciate and take responsibility for the effect that *you* have on those around you. Leaders too often don't consider the effect their influence has on others. They don't see the connection between their own civility—how they treat others—and its effect on trust, productivity, stress, and the bottom line.

Too often leaders are blind to the influence they have on their employees' personal lives. Too many leaders think their behavior affects only those individuals with whom they communicate directly and on a regular basis, in person or virtually. A leader's behavioral style penetrates far deeper than what might be considered its immediate reach. You, as a leader, are not influencing only those folks within earshot, within view, or within reach of your computer messages.

The manner in which you lead is contagious. Your approach in dealing with others spreads throughout the organization—to employees, clients, the community it hopes to serve, and the public at large.

How you lead has an influence on the performance and lives of each person who picks up the phone, walks the halls, totes a product, double-checks accuracy, and ensures quality. Your leadership touches everyone.

ALL EYES ARE ON YOU

Jason Rhode understands this all too well:

> Every single interaction you have with another person leaves that person a little more energized, or a little less. That's true for all of us, but the further up the leadership ladder you are, the greater the leverage you have becomes. Employees notice every single thing you do. Be very mindful of the messages you're sending.[6]

Rhode, the CEO of Cirrus Logic, lobs the responsibility for the culture of your business directly in *your* lap, as a leader. Rhode must be sending the right messages. In 2012, Cirrus Logic ranked ninth on the Great Place to Work Institute's list of top small- and medium-sized companies to work.

Leaders not only set policy, they set tone. Remember, as Rhode says, "Employees notice every single thing you do. Be very mindful of the messages you're sending."

C'S THE DAY LEADERSHIP

Stop reading for a moment and ask yourself:

- Until this moment, what messages have I been sending today?
- Is my message upbeat?
- Do I greet people by name?
- Do I look people in the eye as they pass by?
- Do I play favorites as I move through my environment?
- Do my messages change along with my mood?

Double-check this list first thing upon arrival at work and last thing before heading out. Be sure you make yourself aware of the messages you send, and then adjust as necessary. This adjustment requires practice, attention, and even guidance.

Increasingly in a digital world, our messages go not to a person who's standing close by, but to someone who is in another department, in another building, another part of the country, or another country in the world. Unfortunately, under the pressure of a deadline or in the midst of multitasking, we speedily strike the keys, press "enter"...and then shutter.

It's as though a different personality takes control of our fingertips when we type an email, send a text, or post on social media. As a leader, the messages you send carry added weight. That translates to increased pressure and stress for the recipient of that message. The words you choose, how you position those words, and even the punctuation and capitalization of your message serve as an incentive or deterrent to your request.

Civility is the consistent implementation of respect. Do the messages you send reflect civil leadership?

YOU'RE NOT INVISIBLE

Remember Jason Rhode's statement that employees notice every single thing you do as a leader? They notice where you walk, how you walk, your frowns, your smiles, and what you say, and to whom you say it.

One manufacturing company's new CEO could change everyone's day in a matter of moments as he walked the company's halls and factory lines. Already on edge because of changes in the C-Suite, employees became downcast and nervous as they watched the new boss bark orders, criticize anyone he came upon, and strut through the building like he was there only to be obeyed. No greetings to the men and women doing their jobs, no words of encouragement, no smiles. As a result, everyone wanted to run and hide. And run they did.

In the wake of the CEO's regularly recurring parades with accompanying tirades through the business, devoted employees who'd given years to the company, even those close to retirement, began to look for work elsewhere. They were willing to take the financial risk of looking for a new job because of the toxic environment into which they had suddenly been thrust. Imagine all that knowledge and experience heading out the door. How do you replace that? At what cost? It's this type of incivility by leadership that kicks HR into hyper-drive with exit interviews and paperwork.

Robert Sutton writes in *Good Boss, Bad Boss*, "The top dog sets the tone for how his or her direct reports behave—which reverberates through the system."[7]

> *"The top dog sets the tone for how his or her direct reports behave— which reverberates through the system."*
> —Robert Sutton

The ugly truth about incivility is that it can creep in at any level and set up the perfect conditions for a toxic environment to take hold. One government employee told me that although his supervisor boasted an open-door policy on a regular basis, that same supervisor's habit of walking the halls, head-down, avoiding eye contact and pursing his lips sent an entirely different message. Is it any wonder that the employees never considered going to this supervisor for clarification or mentoring and that there was friction between the leader and his direct reports?

Indifference, rude behavior, lack of awareness, incompatible messages are all ingredients of uncivil leadership, and they undermine what makes a working environment productive and trusting.

TRUST GROWS IN A CULTURE OF CIVILITY

"The toughest thing about the power of trust is that it's very difficult to build and very easy to destroy."[8] Thomas Watson, Sr.'s words underscore the fragility of trust. The former CEO of IBM knew that trust is at the heart of every relationship—professional and personal—and that while it takes time and experience to build, trust evaporates in a blink.

Without civility, there's no trust. Without trust, there's no communication. No civility, no trust, and no communication—the perfect conditions for a toxic environment to take root and grow.

I saw this when I was hired to provide a training on civility with an organization that had increasingly gained a reputation for its toxic environment. Employees flocked to the training, excited to have the opportunity to address the issue head-on. The conference room was packed, and for hours attendees described scenarios in which they'd been dressed down in public, reprimanded on a regular basis, and lectured with condescension and rudeness. Again and again, they explained that as a result, they shut up and shut down. They didn't correct their leaders when they erred—even when it was a matter of safety. These employees, who had once been passionate about their industry, no longer described themselves as loyal—only as stuck. Employment in this industry was hard to come by in the community, so they stayed—for a paycheck and benefits. Employees expressed fear, anger, and the desire for a change.

Trust is always my goal and at the heart of everything I do, whether it's one-on-one coaching or a training session packed with employees, and this training was no different. There was open and honest communication...that is, for most of the morning.

But then, something changed. Twenty minutes before I was to wrap up, the room became quiet, less engaged, and the energy level took a nosedive. Afterward, an attendee approached and asked me whether I had noticed an executive enter from the back of the packed room. This leader's entrance had been quiet and unassuming. The employee said it was this person's unexpected arrival that had been the stimulus to a sudden downward spiral in honest communication. This leader had a reputation for rudeness, hypocrisy, and retaliation. The trust that had inspired vital and honest communication came to a grinding halt because of the unexpected entrance of one person—a leader whose reputation was to choose incivility over civility.

Trust is cultivated and nurtured in an environment of civility in which people feel free to voice their opinions and ideas, even when those opinions and ideas run counter to that of their boss or bosses. When speaking the truth in a toxic environment is rewarded with undermining, demotion, vindictiveness, and aggression, the very character of that business is ravaged.

When leaders stifle differing or even opposing ideas, they reward silence, and that silence can spell disaster. If no one shouts when the ship is taking on water, it won't be long before that ship is at the bottom of the ocean.

Lest you think that a toxic boss is the only reason employees don't speak up, let me be clear that not speaking the truth, no matter why, can be the beginning of the end in the profit and non-profit worlds. Employees sometimes keep their lips sealed in fear of being ostracized for speaking out or for being considered narrow minded or bigoted. Although speaking the truth is valued, the conflicting message we're taught from childhood is that ratting on friends—no matter why—is reprehensible. Tattletales were regarded with disgust early on. However, telling mom that little sis snatched a couple of cookies is a far cry from telling the truth about an individual's unethical or unlawful behavior.

Leaders who value trust, who hold it as something precious to be developed, guarded, and preserved in the workplace, treat people with respect. They understand that civility and trust go hand-in-hand. When trust permeates the atmosphere, people don't walk on eggshells. They create, communicate, and cooperate with a sense of freedom. That creation, communication, and cooperation all lead to a healthier bottom line. The leader who doesn't value or nurture the civility-trust connection treads on unsafe ground and a crumbling foundation. Think bungaroosh!

Remember, the goal of civility is to build connections based on trust!

It's on to the qualities that a civil leader needs to nurture trust that we'll investigate in the next chapter. But please, take a few moments first to study the **Civility Wrap-up** and then incorporate the **C's the Day** pointers in your daily routine.

Civility Wrap-Up

- Leaders unleash civility to develop trust!

- "Employees notice every single thing you do. Be very mindful of the messages you're sending." —Jason Rhode

- "The toughest thing about the power of trust is that it's very difficult to build and very easy to destroy." —Thomas Watson, Sr.

- Leadership is about influencing others.

C's the Day

1. You are an influencer. Decide right now one way in which you can influence those around you in a **positive manner.**

2. As an influencer, consider how your attitude, actions, or approach to relationships may influence others **negatively.** Name one way your influence may not bring out the best in others. What could you do differently?

3. What tone are you setting? How could you change it to improve your environment?

4. Set your email to pop up twice a day to ask you the six questions from page 100. Many of my clients customize these questions. Enjoy the process!

Communicating Character by Exercising Civility

NOTES CHAPTER 8

1 Allison Quigley, "2013 Edelman Trust Barometer Finds a Crisis in Leadership," Edelman Berland, www.edelmanberland.com/uncategorized/2013-edelman-trust-barometer-finds-a-crisis-in-leadership.

2 Lolly Daskall, "30 Quotes on Trust That Will Make You Think," Inc., www.inc.com/lolly-daskal/trust-me-these-30-quotes-about-trust-could-make-a-huge-difference.html.

3 John C. Maxwell, "Goodreads Quotable Quote," www.goodreads.com/quotes/230972-leadership-is-not-about-titles-positions-or-flowcharts-it-is.

4 Linda Kaplan Thaler and Robin Koval, *The Power of Nice: How to Conquer the Business World with Kindness* (New York: Crown Business, 2006), 1.

5 Ibid., 2.

6 "Tips and Secrets from Top CEOs: Gallery," Forbes.com, www.forbes.com/pictures/egee45egekm/jason-rhode-ceo-cirrus.

7 Robert I. Sutton, *Good Boss, Bad Boss* (New York: Business Plus, 2010), 18.

8 Thomas J. Watson, BrainyQuote.com, Xplore Inc. (2015), www.brainyquote.com/quotes/quotes/t/thomasjwa147144.html.

CHAPTER 9
Qualities of the Civil Leader

> *"If you want a quality, act as if you already had it."*
> —William James

Movie star Cary Grant, an elegant purveyor of civility and considered by many as the epitome of a gentleman, once said, "I acted like a gentleman so long I finally became one."[1] Whether or not Grant had ever read William James' quote, he was a living, breathing example of James' message: "If you want a quality, act as if you already had it."[2] Grant's reputation off screen matched that of his characters on screen— he extended respect to all, regardless of status. Whether the person was the president of the United States or the person bussing the table, Grant treated them all kindly. Yet nothing in his turbulent childhood prepared him to be the gentleman that the world would come to know and adore. He had to consciously practice becoming the person he became.

KNOW-HOW AND PRACTICE

We can all learn a valuable lesson from Cary Grant: we can act like a leader—learning the mind-set and skills necessary—for so long that we actually become one. This is not to say that we should fake it in order to use our title or our position of authority to dominate, demand, and direct. Instead, using Grant's example means including the humility to know that to improve oneself, become better, and take oneself to the next level means to study, to practice, and to conduct self-examination.

In this chapter, we'll look at the skills and the characteristics it takes to become a civil leader...the leader whose civility nurtures trust.

THE ABILITY (AND PATIENCE) TO LISTEN

Ernest Hemingway's advice is simple, "When people talk, listen completely. Most people never listen."[3]

He just as well could have said, "Leaders never listen." Often in a hurry, quick to assume they know where the conversation is headed, or impatient for an answer, many leaders fail to take Hemingway's advice. But it's listening that generates trust in those you lead. When you listen, the speaker feels that what he or she is saying matters. Listening is key to communicating respect to the other person.

ASK QUESTIONS

In his book *Good Leaders Ask Great Questions*, leadership expert John Maxwell explains that questions are the most effective means of connecting with people.[4]

As a former television broadcaster, I had the task of connecting with people quickly—within minutes, and sometimes only seconds. I had to connect with the famous, the infamous, and the ordinary guy or gal to learn their stories, their opinions, their reactions, and their observations. The way I connected was through questions. The success of my interviews depended on my asking the right questions, my listening to the responses, and my treating the person on the other side of my microphone with respect. I don't recall a time when that person didn't open up and answer my questions, even when the questions were uncomfortable.

Leaders must ask questions—they don't have all the answers! And sometimes those questions are tough. But civil leaders work to connect and to determine the information and insight they need from others. They do it through listening that is grounded in respect.

CIVIL LEADERS DON'T PLAY FAVORITES

Whether it's the boss's kid or their best bud, civil leaders don't play favorites. Nothing undermines trust faster than when employees see favoritism. Rules must be consistent for everyone.

In his book *Wooden on Leadership*, Coach John Wooden says that leaders must possess two qualities: respect and camaraderie.[5] According to Wooden, it's the leader's job to instill the qualities of respect and camaraderie in their team members as well. Wooden defines camaraderie as a spirit of goodwill that exists between individuals and members of a group—comrades-in-arms.[6]

That camaraderie comes to life when civil leaders are consistent with their expectations, their accountability, and their recognition. They don't have one set of rules for their "faves" and another for everyone else.

CIVIL LEADERS KNOW IT'S A TEAM EFFORT

Another college basketball great is Coach Mike Krzyzewski, whose leadership approach to teamwork has earned him and his team five national titles. Better known as Coach K, the Duke University coach spells out a quality that comes with teamwork: "To me, teamwork is the beauty of our sport, where you have five acting as one. You become *selfless*."[7]

Civil leaders know that they alone are not the source of success. They're humble enough to acknowledge the wisdom, work, and contributions of others. It's that humility and selflessness that guide civil leadership.

CIVIL LEADERS BACK THEIR TEAMS

Nothing builds trust like a leader having their employees' backs. Too often, employees see their leadership pass the buck, point the finger, and not accept blame when leadership is at fault.

Even when leadership is not at fault, but there's been a failure, it may be a leader's place to take the hit. If employees were given the go-ahead, played by the rules, and put out their best efforts, but still came up short, it's important that leadership stand by those individuals. By being nice and polite, but failing to back the people following them, leaders encourage distrust, disengagement, and disloyalty.

Backing your employees is the type of civil leadership that inspires trust, loyalty, and devotion. Civil leaders are wise to take Steven Covey's words to heart: "What you do has far greater impact than what you say."[8]

CIVIL LEADERS HOLD OTHERS ACCOUNTABLE

Don't confuse civility with "niceness" at all costs, because those costs can be enormous. When fear or apathy motivates a leader to play ignorant and look the other way when seeds of incivility, negligence, or unethical behavior are beginning to sprout in their organization's foundation, that's incivility, and as we know from **The 3 C's Rule**— the erosion of character. It's unadulterated incivility that is destructive to working relationships, excellence, and the bottom line. The civil leader expunges the potential for harm by holding accountable those who exhibit bad behavior and perform poorly. Timid leaders who out of fear or indifference don't expect and demand accountability show no respect for their employees who are playing by the rules and working to build a trusting workplace. Not holding oneself and others accountable quickly leads to a toxic environment.

CIVIL LEADERS ADMIT WHEN THEY'RE WRONG

John Maxwell sums up this quality in one short sentence. "A true leader is one who is humble enough to admit [his] mistakes."[9] We all make mistakes, and leaders aren't exempt from apologizing, but even the manner in which leaders admit *mea culpa* defines them as civil or uncivil.

When Netflix increased its subscription prices by 60 percent and split its DVD and streaming options, thousands of its customers took to social media to complain, the stock price tanked, and more than 800 thousand subscribers dumped Netflix. Two months later, Netflix CEO Reed Hastings issued a public apology on the company's website. Netflix's 24 million subscribers did not react with "apology accepted."[10] Instead, many of the 13 thousand people who went on the Netflix blog described the apology as arrogant, condescending, and manipulative. Ouch! The negative reaction to the request for forgiveness was blamed in part for taking too long—it took two months for the company to issue an apology.

Professor Daniel Diermeier of Northwestern University's Kellogg School of Management concluded it best: "If it takes too long, the people always believe it's calculated. When it's calculated, then it's worse than not apologizing at all."[11]

Civil leaders admit they're wrong, and then quickly do so with respect and integrity.

CIVIL LEADERS DON'T POUNCE

The former CEO of General Electric Jack Welch says, "When people make mistakes, the last thing they need is discipline. It's time for encouragement and confidence building. The job at this point is to restore self-confidence. I think 'piling on' when someone is down is one of the worst things any of us can do."[12]

Obviously, Welch is not speaking about the person who repeatedly makes mistakes because of poor performance, an unwilling attitude, or a mismatch of skills. But as a former leader of thousands of employees worldwide, Welch knows that humans make mistakes, and when they do it's an opportunity for a leader to coach his or her subordinates to better results and from a position of support.

Remember that Jason Rhode said, "Employees notice every single thing you do." Leaders must develop keen self-awareness because employees not only notice every single thing their leaders do, they feel every single thing their leaders do. If acting with respect, the leader is helping to develop and build a foundation of trust.

Civil Leaders...

- Listen
- Ask questions
- Don't play favorites
- Know it's a team effort
- Back their teams

- Aren't afraid to hold others (and themselves) accountable
- Admit they may be wrong
- Don't pounce

In the next chapter, we'll learn how civil leaders spell it out. One of the greatest obstacles to trust and a contributor to a toxic environment is confusion. We'll take a look at clarity in just a moment, but first let's review our **Civility Wrap-up**. Then please be sure to **C's the Day**!

Civility Wrap-Up

Civil leaders...

1. Begin the work by studying and then putting into practice the skills and mental mindset of a leader.

2. Don't have to have the last word.

3. Treat each and every person with respect.

4. Know they are not responsible for all the success.

5. Support those they lead.

6. Hold themselves and others accountable.

7. Admit it when they make a mistake.

8. Don't discipline when someone fails; they support.

C's the Day

1. Ask yourself whether you are just doing the job, or are you studying and working to become a better civil leader. If yes, what are you doing now that you should continue? If no, what is your plan to start? Be specific.

2. Select one skill from items 1–4 in the **Civility Wrap-up**. Write down that skill and how you will learn to improve your skills in that area.

3. Select one skill from items 5–8 in the **Civility Wrap-up**. Write down that skill and how you will learn to improve your skills in that area.

Communicating Character by Exercising Civility

NOTES CHAPTER 9

1 Marjabelle Young Stewart, *Commonsense Etiquette* (New York: St. Martin's Press, 1999), 8.

2 William James, BrainyQuote.com, Xplore Inc. (2015), www.brainyquote.com/quotes/quotes/w/williamjam163787.html.

3 Ernest Hemingway, BrainyQuote.com, Xplore Inc. (2015), www.brainyquote.com/quotes/quotes/e/ernesthemi383060.html.

4 John Maxwell, *Good Leaders Ask Great Questions* (New York: Hachette Books, 2014),7.

5 John Wooden and Steve Jamison, *Wooden on Leadership* (New York: McGraw-Hill, 2005), 25.

6 Ibid.

7 "Basketball Plays and Tips," www.basketball-plays-and-tips.com/mike-krzyzewski-quotes.html (emphasis added).

8 Kevin Kruse, "100 Best Quotes on Leadership," Forbes.com, www.forbes.com/sites/kevinkruse/2012/10/16/quotes-on-leadership.

9 John Maxwell, *Good Leaders Ask Great Questions* (New York: Hachette Books, 2014).

10 William D. Cohan, "Seeing Red," Vanity Fair (February 22, 2102), www.vanityfair.com/news/2012/02/netflix-201202.

11 Robert Channick and Corilyn Shropshire, "Netflix Walks Fine Line with Apology," Chicago Tribune, September 19, 2011, http://articles.chicagotribune.com/2011-09-19/business/chi-netflix-to-split-off-rename-dvd-service-ceo-i-screwed-up-20110919_1_netflix-subscribers-reed-hastings-apology.

12 Jack Welch with John A. Byrne, *Jack: Straight from the Gut* (New York: Warner Business Books, 2001).

CHAPTER 10
Why Leaders Must Care

> *"Play fair. Don't hit people. Say you're sorry when you hurt somebody."*
> —Robert Fulghum

These three rules are spelled out so simply in *All I Really Need to Know I Learned in Kindergarten*: "Play fair. Don't hit people. Say you're sorry when you hurt somebody."[1] They seem so straight forward, right? The problem is that we don't play fair, we do hit people—if you don't believe me, check out social media—and we seldom apologize (and if we do, it's rarely with genuine culpability or sincerity).

This simple trio of rules isn't any easier in business than on the playground. In fact, the bottom line of business seems to be the perfect excuse to cast aside the rules. That's where the civil leader comes in. He or she must ensure that everyone plays fair—especially the leader. It's up to the leader to safeguard the "no hitting rule" whether the hits are verbal, strategic, or physical. And when it comes to apologizing, it's the leader who should show how it's done.

Why should a leader care about modeling civil leadership? I give you the following five reasons to care about taking the lead in guaranteeing a civil workplace:

- Money
- Incompetence
- Safety

- Ignorance
- Set-up for Failure

Let's take a look at each concern and its effect.

MONEY: YOUR BOTTOM LINE TAKES A NOSEDIVE

A commitment to keeping your bottom line in the black makes civility a must. Incivility has huge financial costs, and it's not just the obvious potential of lawsuits. Its costs are incremental and insidious.

Incivility and poor performance go hand in hand. As Christine Pearson and Christine Porath detail in *The Cost of Bad Behavior*, targets of incivility don't have to file a formal complaint to cause chaos and disruption, they just disengage and/or retaliate. Their work is left incomplete or, if completed, it's of poor quality. Employees begin to move in a dance of avoiding one another and increasingly become out of sync. Loyalty and trust are missing in action. Pearson and Porath's numbers are shocking to read, but they explain the toll a disrespectful business environment takes on the financial well-being of any business. When people became targets of incivility:

- 48 percent intentionally decreased work effort
- 47 percent intentionally decreased time at work
- 38 percent intentionally decreased work quality
- 80 percent lost work time worrying about the incident
- 63 percent lost time avoiding the offender
- 66 percent said their performances declined
- 78 percent said their commitment to the organization declined[2]

It's not so hard to track increasing sick days; it's more difficult to quantify disengagement and lack of commitment. It's also difficult to "catch" incivility in the act.

Think back to junior high. When your teacher was suddenly called from the classroom for even moments, chaos was unleashed. Goodbye teacher, hello yelling, hurling any item within reach, and talking trash about your teacher or another classmate. But just as quickly, as you and your buddies heard the teacher's footsteps approaching, silence took hold, and you all resumed being perfect little angels.

It's not any different in most workplaces. Enter the leader, and squabbling colleagues begin to cooperate, focus on the project at hand, and give the impression that all is well. Too often, leaders are ignorant of the chaos, negativity, and growing resentment percolating just below the surface. It's not until HR announces that there's been a complaint that the issue comes to light.

As if that's not bad enough, when incivility takes the reins, people lose focus. They constantly anticipate the next attack. Literally and figuratively, these targets look over their shoulders, unable to move toward any goal at work. Concentration, memory, and focus get hammered! Pearson and Porath's research shows that concentration suffers when participants of their experiment even *imagined* an uncivil event:

- Short-term memories suffer. Participants recalled nearly 20 percent less.
- Participants who experienced incivility were 30 percent less creative.
- Participants who experienced incivility produced 25 percent fewer ideas.
- The ideas of participants who experienced incivility were less diverse.[3]

As you'd expect, incivility alienates helpfulness. But just how much incivility breeds disrespect may surprise you.

> When people were treated uncivilly, their inclination to assist others dropped, too. In the first study, in which no incivility had occurred, 90 percent of participants helped pick up something that had been intentionally dropped. But when the experimenter insulted a confederate [a colleague who was actually an actor for the purpose of research] for being late, only 35 percent offered any help. In the second study, 73 percent of those who hadn't

experienced incivility volunteered to lend a hand. But when a confederate was rude to participants who were trying to find where the study was taking place, only 24 percent of those who had been treated uncivilly offered to help.[4]

With people working at a small percentage of their potential, unable to think clearly about the work at hand, and moving away rather than toward a collaborative relationship, is it any wonder that incivility chips away at the financial and emotional foundation of any business?

Civil leaders take full responsibility for a workplace environment that protects and promotes respectful behavior, which in turn protects and promotes the bottom line.

YOUR MANAGERS ARE INCOMPETENT

OK, not all of your managers are incompetent, but 82 percent of them are! According to Gallup Research, **most managers are miscast**. Furthermore, **"18 percent of current managers have the high talent[5] required of their role, while 82 percent do not have high talent."** Gallup goes on to report that only 30 percent of U.S. managers are engaged.[6]

What Gallup is telling us is that most American managers are both miscast and disengaged. No wonder there's not a direct line between management and success! Organizations settle for the wrong people in positions of management.

Why would any business settle for a bad choice in management? The reasons are endless: Sometimes leadership promotes best buddies or family members—who have no qualifications for the job. Sometimes decision makers are threatened by an employee who is a rising star. To punish that employee, someone less capable is promoted over them. Laziness can prompt a quick hire—"we just need a warm body to manage the department. It basically runs itself." Ha! Decision makers, too often, don't understand the job sufficiently well (if at all) to hire not only for the right skills, but for the right attitudes. There's also pressure to fill according to guidelines and a lack of patience or time to find the accurate match. Filling the spot with a promotion based solely on longevity with the organization is not uncommon. Employees who hate managing people are dubbed as managers and then remain there without coaching or training despite the mismatch. The culture may be such a mess that civility acumen is not a consideration. Poor managers hire poor managers. Unable to lead, inspire, and be effective, those managers disengage. Before long, their direct reports follow their manager's lead and disengage as well.

Although civility may not be the complete solution for reversing these depressing statistics, civility can go a long way to steering a team in the right direction. It's easier to learn, repair, resuscitate, and ignite a strategy for success in an environment of respect.

EMOTIONAL SAFETY

People suffer in a toxic environment. The emotional toll that rudeness, disrespect, and poor leadership take on an individual translates to a physical toll. Writing for Forbes.com, Amy Rees Anderson describes her observations of employees working in toxic environment under poor leadership and the obvious effects the dysfunctionality had on its employees.[7] If there had been a "before" photo taken when the employee entered this atmosphere and an "after" photo months into it, Anderson says the physical manifestations would be staggering. Anderson said that she watched as one by one, each employee resigned, despite having good salaries and fabulous benefits, without even having a future job in hand. The toxic fallout was too much for their self-respect and their health.

The National Institute for Occupational Safety and Health estimates that 40 percent of the U.S. workforce is affected by stress, making it the top cause of worker disability.[8]

It's not unusual for leaders to talk about caring for their employees, but civil leaders go way beyond talk. They show they care by ensuring that employees know they care. Incivility is not tolerated in any form.

In his book *The 21 Irrefutable Laws of Leadership*, John Maxwell says that leaders must value people and demonstrate that they care in such a way that their followers know it. Maxwell continues by describing an episode in his own workplace:

> Dan Reiland, who was my right-hand man for many years, is an excellent leader and values people highly. But when he first came to work for me, he didn't show it. One day when he was new on the job, I was chatting with some people in the lobby, and Dan came in, briefcase in hand. Dan walked right past all of us without saying a word and went straight down the hall toward his office. I was astounded. How could a leader walk right by a group of people he worked with and not even say hello to them? I quickly excused myself from the conversation I was having and followed Dan to his office.
>
> "Dan," I asked after greeting him, "how could you walk right past everybody like that?"
>
> "I've got a lot of work to do today," Dan answered, "and really want to get started."
>
> Dan," I said, "you just walked past your work. Never forget that leadership is about people." Dan cared about people and wanted to serve them as a leader. He just didn't show it.[9]

The civil leader has to become aware of his or her own behavior. Self-awareness is absolutely critical to civil leadership. Dan's sprinting toward his office without so much as a nod to his colleagues certainly failed to show respect and care. It also showed a lack of appreciation for other people in the organization, yet appreciation is one of the first steps to cultivating trust.

John Maxwell nipped even the first hint of incivility in the bud, knowing as all civil leaders must, that incivility allowed to run rampant produces suffering.

YOUR EMPLOYEES DON'T KNOW HOW TO BE CIVIL

We know civility when we see it. We know what civility feels like when we experience it. The problem is, we just don't know how to be civil.

Research shows that one of the leading causes for incivility in the workplace is that we don't know how to be civil.[10] This element that is foundational to customer service and positive and productive workplace relationships is a mystery to many. The civil leader removes the mystery when he or she spells out the civil culture for the workplace.

Greg Gianforte is the founder of RightNow Technologies, a cloud-based tech company that he launched in an extra bedroom when he moved to Bozeman, Montana—a university town not exactly considered a hot spot for technology. Under Gianforte's leadership, the company grew quickly until it reached 1,100 employees. RightNow went public in 2004 and was bought by Oracle Corporation in 2011 for $1.8 billion.

Gianforte told me that as RightNow began to grow, "we had a very specific culture definition. We worked very deliberately in inculcating that culture into the organization."[11] The company's four-part culture statement was:

1. Customers are the reason we exist
2. Integrity in everything we do
3. Growth of the individual
4. Expect success

Gianforte said that he knew they had the culture definition correct, but as the company grew by 30 to 40 employees per month, with 22 offices world-wide, the definition turned out to be insufficient to clarify expected behaviors in the workplace. Those four tenets of culture were not specific enough. No one could argue with the values, but exactly what does that culture look like? How do we model it?

A committee tried to translate those high-level concepts into tangible steps, but their solutions still didn't give employees what Gianforte called a "road map to decide should I turn right or turn left at a given fork in the road."[12]

Gianforte, as CEO, decided to take on the task himself because, as he says, "One of the primary responsibilities of leadership is to define this corporate culture."[13] Gianforte started with the end-game in mind and worked backward to build the desired culture. "If we've gotten the culture right, what are the day-to-day individual behaviors that will manifest themselves?"[14]

Gianforte came up with about 12 to 15 behaviors, which he admits were way too many; however, they were much more specific and therefore, actionable! Here are a few:

- We show up to meetings on time. (Not coming to a meeting on time shows disrespect for those who do.)
- Everyone has dirt under their fingernails. (Everyone is a worker; there is no one here just keeping score.)
- Every job in this business is critical to our success. (Gianforte explained that he finds a noble attribute to each and every job in the organization; the janitor's job is just as important as the CEO's or VP of Marketing's.)

Gianforte's message to leaders is as concrete as that of Jason Rhode's: as leaders, one of your primary jobs, if not goal number one, is to define the corporate culture. If your culture is not based on the consistent implementation of respect, you are not building on a rock-solid foundation. If each and every job in a business is critical to success, each and every job deserves the respect of all members of that company.

Leaders, your job is to define, design, and implement your corporate culture.

YOU SET UP YOUR EMPLOYEES FOR FAILURE

Great leaders keep taking it a step further. As Gianforte's road map shows, leaders not only describe the vision, they zero in on the details. Unless everyone on a team knows specifically what to do, how to execute, and can consistently deliver in a systematic way, team members are left confused, off balance, and primed to disengage.

The fact is that success is in the details. If we coached a basketball team the way many leaders coach their employees, we'd just round them up, point to the court, toss the basketball to someone in the group whom we designate as captain, and then tell them to "go out there and win!" We set them up not only to lose, but to fail miserably, and often publicly.

Imagine the consequence if the coach doesn't take the time to teach dribbling, shooting, passing, or blocking. What if the coach doesn't bother explaining to the players how to behave when fouled, when the ref makes a bad call, or when the scoreboard shows a bleak picture? No coach could be so negligent and then expect a win! An excellent performance demands specific guidance and great attention to detail.

Think of civility as the ultimate win for a company's culture!

I again look to the wisdom of Coach John Wooden, whose teams won 10 NCAA national championships in 12 years. He was awarded the highest civilian honor in 2003, the Presidential Medal of Freedom. In writing about what led to his success in his and Steve Jamison's book, *Wooden on Leadership*, the coach underscores his attention to details. His players never had to guess what his expectations included, on the court or off. And his players never could have imagined the lengths or level of detail that Coach Wooden went to in order to ensure that his expectations were clear.

Lynn Shackleford, who played on UCLA's varsity basketball team from 1967 through 1969 and won three national championships, described the first team meeting he ever attended at the university. Sitting next to him was Kareem Abdul-Jabbar, "the guy who had been the most coveted high school player in America..."[15] Shackleford described his initial reaction of shock to Coach Wooden's first words to the team:

> "Gentlemen," he said, "Welcome. Let's get down to business. I want to remind each one of you of a few important rules we have here at UCLA. Number one: keep your fingernails trimmed. Number two: Keep your hair short. Number three: Keep your jersey tucked into your trunks at all times." He looked around the room for a moment and then added solemnly: "Am I clear?"
>
> I wondered, "Is he making a joke?" But there was no laughter, not even smiles, from any varsity players. They knew better. Nevertheless, I couldn't understand why he was wasting his time on stuff like that.
>
> As the months—eventually years (and three more national championships)—went by, I came to recognize that "stuff like that" was part of the genius in his leadership. There was logic to every move. Details of fingernails, hair, and jerseys led to

details for running plays, handling the ball, and everything else—hundreds of small things done right.

Everything was related to everything else; nothing was left to chance; it all had to be done well. Sloppiness was not allowed in anything; not in passing, shooting, or trimming your fingernails and tucking in a jersey.

Coach Wooden taught that great things can only be accomplished by doing the little things right. Doing things right became a habit with us.[16]

Do you see his detail? Coach Wooden's expectations were based on precise training, which produced consistent results. And his result was success. I know what you're thinking, "Diana, you're telling me to micromanage!" Not in the least. Coach Wooden expected his players to watch, learn, and follow through. I'm sure the coach didn't hover over his players as they suited up day after day, practice after practice, and game after game. The coach didn't interrogate them about every minute detail. He didn't need to micromanage. He taught the specifics. He was thorough. He watched to see what worked and what didn't. His expectation was that of excellence. Leaders, are you paying attention to the details? Have you defined your civil corporate culture? What is it? Does everyone know the details of your corporate culture? Are you an example of that civility day in and day out?

Leaders who have a distinct picture of success paint that image so that each person understands clearly the expectations for the culture. If you mean to consistently implement respect, you can't assume that everyone understands how that respect looks, sounds, and feels. Your corporate culture, whether your workplace is composed of thousands, hundreds, or just a couple of employees, sends a message to each of the senses. It has a look, a sound, a feel, a smell—and sometimes even a taste. If you think I'm exaggerating, take a look at studies on the importance of wall color and scents wafting through the building. If all of this seems inconsequential, you may find that your clients and employees are leaving with a bad taste in their mouths—even though you're not in the restaurant business!

KNOWLEDGE IS TAKEN FOR GRANTED

One of the most common refrains that we hear in business after someone makes a mistake that costs time, reputation, and dollars is, "He (or she) should have known better!"

Really? Did you as a leader make your expectations clear? Did you define and describe the required behavior? Did you spell out the details? Or did you just assume that the individual knew how to communicate respectfully, dress appropriately, respond with patience, and hold direct reports accountable without condescension, rudeness, or sarcasm?

Coach Wooden didn't take for granted any player's knowledge...even when it came to lessons most of us learn in kindergarten, like putting on your shoes and socks. Imagine this scene: You're the coach, in a gym, surrounded by athletes who were the super jocks in high school and college. They tower over you; they're younger and cocky. And you begin to tell them how to put on their shoes and socks!

That's exactly what Wooden described and displayed for his teams. Wooden would tell his teams to sit down and remove their shoes and socks...as he did the same. Barefoot and surrounded by remarkable athletes, he showed them how to put on their socks so that there were no blister-causing wrinkles, no painful overlap of material, no shoelaces that could become untied and trip a player—nothing that could get in the way of their playing their best.

When leaders expect follow-through without guidance, training, and clarity, leaders set up their employees and their teams for failure. Coach Wooden ensured that his players knew better. Lack of attention and the failure to train details never got in the way of Coach Wooden's teams' success. Granted, the details necessary to win college basketball championships will not be the details needed for your business to excel in the marketplace; however, as Wooden said, "identifying and perfecting those [details] that apply to our situation is a duty entrusted to those in leadership. Being negligent in this area breaks the trust."[17]

EINSTEIN KNEW CIVILITY

"It has become appallingly obvious that our technology has exceeded our humanity."[18] This quote, attributed to Albert Einstein, serves as a stark reminder that it's our humanity that must be preserved at all costs.

Although Einstein was referring to atomic warfare when he uttered these words, I like to think he may have seen the writing on the wall regarding a future where smart technology isolates us and replaces our interactions with other human beings. Technological interactions—even if you're using emoticons—are worlds apart from human communication, and we seem to be losing our humanity as our abilities to relate to other people erode, just like Einstein observed. Technology enables us to be the sun in our own universe—selfies, anyone?—thereby belittling those around us, intentionally or not. When we're number one, why should we care about the other guy's suffering? We, as a society, are losing our hearts and possibly our minds as well. Einstein knew the value of civility, of humanity. Shouldn't we do the same?

The civil leader takes full responsibility for the organization's civil environment! How? By implementing structure and systems that bring awareness, accountability, and appreciation for civility. But to be able to be civil in the workplace, one must exercise one's own civil self, early and often. And that's where we are headed in Part IV.

You know the drill: please review the **Civility Wrap-up**, and then please **C's the Day**!

Civility Wrap-Up

- Play fair.

- Targets in an uncivil environment aren't producing. They're struggling just to focus.

- If you permit incivility, time is lost, productivity is lost, your employees are lost.

- Only 30 percent of U.S. managers are engaged per Gallup. Don't be a statistic!

- You truly help people and their emotional health when you commit to a civil environment.

- You're the teacher. Teach civility by modeling civility!

C's the Day

Consider Coach John Wooden's attention to detail. To some it could be considered micromanaging; to others it is clearly outlining your expectations. How could your attention to detail transform your environment into one that is more civil? How can you walk the line between expressing your expectations and not micromanaging?

Communicating Character by Exercising Civility

NOTES CHAPTER 10

1 Robert Fulghum, *All I Really Need to Know I Learned in Kindergarten* (New York: Ballantine Books, 1986).

2 Christine Pearson and Christine Porath, *The Cost of Bad Behavior: How Incivility Is Damaging Your Business and What to Do about It* (New York: Portfolio, 2009), 55.

3 Ibid., 57–58.

4 Ibid., 58–9.

5 Tim Gould, "Are 82% of Your Managers Less Than Competent? Gallup Thinks So," April 3, 2015, www.hrmorning.com/are-82-of-your-managers-less-than-competent-gallup-thinks-so.

6 Cara Eccleston, "Gallup Rules 9 of 10 Managers Incompetent," May 12, 2015, http://careerlink.com/lp/gallup-rules-9-of-10-managers-incompetent.

7 Amy Rees Anderson, "Coping in a Toxic Work Environment," Forbes.com, www.forbes.com/sites/amyanderson/2013/06/17/coping-in-a-toxic-work-environment.

8 Ricky W. Griffin and Anne M. O'Leary-Kelly, *The Dark Side of Organizational Behavior* (Hoboken, NJ: Pfeiffer, 2004), 73–74.

9 John C. Maxwell, *The 21 Irrefutable Laws of Leadership* (Nashville, TN: Thomas Nelson, 1998 and 2007), 53–54.

10 Christine Pearson and Christine Porath, *The Cost of Bad Behavior: How Incivility Is Damaging Your Business and What to Do about It* (New York: Portfolio, 2009), 144.

11 Greg Gianforte (founder and former CEO of RightNow Technologies) in phone conversation with the author, March 3, 2015.

12 Ibid.

13 Ibid.

14 Ibid.

15 John Wooden and Steve Jamison, *Wooden on Leadership* (New York: McGraw-Hill, 2005), 148.

16 Ibid., 148–149.

17 Ibid., 145.

18 Albert Einstein, BrainyQuote.com, Xplore Inc. (2015), www.brainyquote.com/quotes/quotes/a/alberteins161262.html.

PART IV: THE CIVIL SELF

CHAPTER 11
Exercise Your Civil Self

I run my consulting company on the principle that you **Communicate your *Character* by how you exercise your *Civility*—The 3 C's**. Essential to this concept is the focus on what we call civility and just how we exercise it. Our civility expresses our values. Our civility sends a message to each person in our lives with whom we have contact. That message is positive or negative, seldom neutral. How we treat our colleagues tells them who we are at our core. How we behave with our friends and families announces our values. How we treat strangers reveals our heart. If this weren't true, social media wouldn't light up with videos of a stranger rewriting the sign of a blind man begging on the street in order to soften the hearts and open the purses of passers-by. We "like" by the millions the videos of men and women sitting down to make music with a homeless man. And videos go viral when we see what can take place when a stranger brings a sandwich and a bottle of water to a homeless fellow.

That implementation of respect, consistently expressed regardless of another's circumstance, is civility expressed. Civility touches the heart of another—even if subconsciously—and civility rarely leaves us where it found us.

CIVILITY WITHIN

They say that charity begins at home. So does civility. It begins within one's self; it grows within our own hearts and minds. But civility is a funny thing. Bring up the word, and everyone looks away from themselves. In other words, we tend to check out whether everyone else is exercising civility. As far as our own civility, too often we give ourselves a pass. Believe me, I'm guilty of it, too. As someone who is constantly working to keep my impatience in check, I can easily come up with excuses for why I was short with the customer service rep who answered my questions by phone or why I drove close enough to read every bumper sticker on the car that's going five miles below the speed limit in the passing lane.

I ask that right now you make a commitment. As you read Part IV: The Civil Self, don't waste a moment wondering how this information affects anyone else. This is about *you*. Exercising civility is a lot like committing to an exercise program. When you walk into the gym, only you can do the work. No one else can lift the weights, run the treadmill, and eat a healthy diet but you. The benefits that you want to see and will see only come with your commitment and your follow through.

Don't get me wrong, working out with others helps immensely. Although colleagues and coaches can't do the work for us, they really can motivate us—sometimes with their words or hints, sometimes with the competition of knowing that if they can do it, we sure as heck can, too!

When I was in my twenties, I took up jogging. Honestly, I hated every moment and every step at first. I asked a friend to join me on my new 6:00 a.m. daily routine. Every morning, I'd meet Scott to run those city blocks. He'd push me just a bit farther each morning through humor or a wicked challenge. Within a month, those steps became miles, and within a couple of months, every day we met to put in six miles. And it felt great! While Scott made the jog more fun, he couldn't do the work for me. I was the one who had to put one foot in front of the other block after block, mile after mile.

Like my morning jog, civility isn't always easy; but like daily commitment, civility pays off! The discipline, strength, and flexibility that result from civility pay huge dividends.

CIVILITY WORKS BOTH WAYS

The focus on our civil self is two-fold: how we exercise civility toward others and how we exercise civility toward ourselves. They go hand in hand; after all, how can we treat another with civility if we don't treat ourselves with civility? If we don't have respect for ourselves, how can we begin the process of demonstrating respect for others? If we're not kind to ourselves, how can we be truly kind to others? If we're not generous with ourselves, how can we be generous toward others?

Let me be very clear, I'm not talking about giving ourselves a free pass or demanding special treatment. I am talking about the destructive behavior of berating ourselves, telling ourselves that we don't measure up, or playing the comparison game. That self-bullying doesn't set us up for positive, constructive, and healthy interactions with others. In fact, it's the perfect way for us to launch into negative, defensive, and passive-aggressive behavior.

 Neither self-adulation nor self-bullying leads to the development and maintenance of our civil self.

Neither self-adulation nor self-bullying leads to the development and maintenance of our civil self. The civil self demands self-respect, which leads to confidence, commitment, and respectful behavior toward others. The civil self also demands work.

For our sakes, if not for others, we have to confront self-bullying and self-adulation with decisive action. The actions we take to improve our civil self are exactly the same actions we take when we want to get into better physical shape: diet and exercise.

THE CIVILITY WORKOUT

Now, don't come up with the excuses before we even get started. I'm going to take you into the civility gym and we are going to get you into civil shape. I've laid out Part IV as the Civility Workout. Consider me your Civility Personal Trainer—I'll be here with you every step of the way. First, we begin with an assessment of your body of civility right now. Then you'll take an inventory of your emotional and mental pantry, and start tossing out the trash. Anything that doesn't strengthen your civil self gets dumped. There are eight nasty qualities that are as toxic as any calorie-laden, chemically infused, sugar-charged junk food, and you're going to see how they're contributing to your less-than-civil—perhaps, even toxic—behavior.

Don't worry, I'm not going to leave you craving junk, and not help you develop an appetite for the good stuff. I cover those qualities that nourish the very best in us and contribute to our healthy environment in the next chapter.

Exercising civility is an exercise program like any other. It takes commitment, it takes discipline, and it takes a willingness to change some poor—and maybe even nasty—habits that keep us from getting into great civil shape. It means re-thinking goals, or perhaps, beginning to create goals that translate to meaningful change.

I won't kid you. Civility takes work—consistent work, ongoing awareness, and a dedication to make a change that means a better life, not only for yourself, but for those with whom you work, live, and engage.

And like any exercise program, it starts with measuring where you are right now. Let's go.

AN HONEST LOOK AT YOURSELF

The first day at the gym is the worst! The trainer walks up to you, smiles, and hands you a clipboard with a form attached. On that form are questions—lots of questions...*personal* questions. Just scanning the questions makes you wince. Height (*at least that's one number you can't work to change*), weight (*too much*), strength (*too little*), flexibility (*you're kidding right?*), endurance (*you're already out of breath, and you're just holding the pencil*).

Then there are the performance questions: how long can you run on the treadmill? (*Are we measuring in minutes or seconds?*) Can you bend over and touch your toes? (*You're already coming up with excuses for why that question is stupid and way too personal!*) How many pushups can you complete? (*You're still working on your first one!*)

Although often embarrassing, even painful, that appraisal of where we are at the moment gives us a definitive point from which to start. It's the trainer's job to help us define our goals, guide us to reach them, and along the way, lend encouragement, tips, and perhaps even some prodding. With the assessment in hand, the goals defined, and the ongoing coaching, it still remains up to us to do the work to make the necessary changes. I often marvel at the participants on the TV hit show *America's Biggest Loser*. They're dissatisfied, sometimes even disgusted, with their physical and perhaps emotional shape. They want to be in better control of themselves in order to achieve healthier lives. They want to make the changes necessary to create positive, loving, and enduring relationships. And they're willing to go through a rigorous and very public boot camp to reach their goals.

It's not much different when it comes to civility. At first glance, we're not talking about pounds, exercise schedules, or dietary regimens. We're talking about the consistent implementation of respect. The questions may be different; however, they still involve strength, flexibility, and heart-sourced endurance.

Are you resilient under stress? Are you flexible and able to respond consistently with civility when your team is depending on you to make it to the group's goal? Or do you jump off the emotional treadmill, roll your eyes, throw in your towel, and head outside?

Please take a few moments, and maybe a deep breath. Determine how you measure up when it comes to your own Civility Quotient (CQ). Be honest—you're here to learn, get stronger, become more flexible and more resilient, and transform yourself into an even more robust civil self.

CIVILITY QUOTIENT ASSESSMENT

Please circle the number that best describes you. Circle 5 if you believe you excel in this area. Circle 1 if you think you need a lot of work, or it's not important to you. Of the 28 questions, there's the potential for a low score of 28 (You've got some work to do) and a high score of 140 (Mother Teresa would be proud of you!).

Strength

I consider civility a high priority.	1	2	3	4	5
I have the know-how to be polite even when others are not.	1	2	3	4	5
I don't let people take advantage of me.	1	2	3	4	5
I can laugh at myself.	1	2	3	4	5
I can assess my strengths with objectivity and humility.	1	2	3	4	5
I can assess my weaknesses without making excuses.	1	2	3	4	5
I can make mistakes without beating myself up.	1	2	3	4	5
No matter my "internal" mood, I can be positive in the workplace.	1	2	3	4	5
I'm self-aware and can move from uncivil to civil.	1	2	3	4	5
I expect to be treated with respect.	1	2	3	4	5
I don't berate myself.	1	2	3	4	5

Flexibility (Patience)

I can physically and emotionally feel the difference when I move toward civility.	1	2	3	4	5
I'm slow to take offense.	1	2	3	4	5
If someone is rude to me I don't respond to them rudely.	1	2	3	4	5
I give others the benefit of the doubt: colleagues, supervisors, direct-reports, customers.	1	2	3	4	5
"Just do what I tell you; don't ask why!" is not my way of doing business.	1	2	3	4	5
If my idea doesn't "win," I still work to promote the ideas of others.	1	2	3	4	5
I can listen to criticism and consider whether it has merit.	1	2	3	4	5

Cardio (The Heart)

I feel different when I'm cognizant of being civil.	1	2	3	4	5
I take care of myself physically: diet, sleep, exercise.	1	2	3	4	5
My intake of TV, radio, videos, social media and reading puts me in a better place emotionally.	1	2	3	4	5
I try to understand the perspective of others.	1	2	3	4	5
When someone is rude to me, I don't dwell on it and I let it go.	1	2	3	4	5
I listen to others.	1	2	3	4	5
I ask follow-up questions to ensure clarity.	1	2	3	4	5
I thank my colleagues, direct-reports, supervisors, and customers.	1	2	3	4	5
I regularly display appreciation to other people for their work.	1	2	3	4	5
I don't let gossip or hearsay affect the way I interact with someone.	1	2	3	4	5

With your assessment in hand, you should have an idea of what you'll see when you stand in front of the mirror of civility. Do you detect in your reflection a carved and powerful musculature of behaviors that demonstrate tolerance, thoughtfulness, and even tact? Or are you just a bit flabby in those areas? Is your flexibility such that you could lead a yoga class, or does a look in the mirror of civility reveal rigidity and a sense of self-entitlement? And what about that cardio—you know, the heart piece of the assessment? Do you try to consistently see the other person's perspective?

CIVILITY: A MATTER OF CHOICE

In his book *Good to Great*, Jim Collins writes, "Greatness is not a function of circumstance. Greatness, it turns out, is largely a matter of conscious choice."[1]

 Being civil is largely a matter of conscious choice.

It's the same with civility. Being civil is not a function of circumstance. Being civil is largely a matter of conscious choice. Each of us has the opportunity to make that choice day-by-day, moment by moment. Granted, sometimes it's an easy choice—like when the person is a client with a big, fat account or the colleague who agrees with every idea you have. But far too frequently, the circumstance involves someone whom we find disagreeable or a situation contains something we consider untenable.

Still we have to make the choice, and we know the choice has to be civility. So what gets in our way? More often than not, we make the choices that are easy, but not necessarily healthy, for our personal and professional relationships. It's so much easier to give in to an emotional outburst rather than demonstrate respect for another person. In terms of our diet, there's a lot that you and I ingest that needs to be eliminated from our diet in order for us to get into Civil Shape:

- Excuses
- Entitlement
- Rumination
- Authenticity
- Unhealthy Choices
- Our Personal Intake of Garbage
- No Systems in Place
- Ignorance

Excuses

Have you ever started an exercise program only to come up with excuses by the fourth day of why you just can't make it to the gym? I have. The excuses include no time, no energy, sore muscles, dirty gym clothes, my favorite piece of workout equipment is never free, and of course let's not forget, a bad hair day.

Dieting is no different! What we should eat is too expensive, takes too much time, isn't readily available, and isn't always easy to fix. There's no guarantee that all the extra fuss will be worth it and that everyone else will appreciate our new approach to healthy living. In fact, sometimes we discard the healthy menu because it means changing friends who have contempt for anything other than their burgers and beers regimen.

When excuses come between you and your civil self, ditch them! They make attaining any goal, whether it's your civil self or your healthier self, next to impossible to achieve.

Entitlement

There's nothing like a sense of entitlement to put up a roadblock to showing consideration for others. If you've been raised to believe that you deserve to be the center of the world's attention, then the idea of looking out for others may seem like an absurd notion. Entitlement and the self-esteem movement appear to go hand-in-hand. In her seminal book, *Generation Me: Why Today's Young Americans Are More Confident, Assertive, Entitled—and More Miserable Than Ever Before*, Dr. Jean Twenge, herself a member of the Me Generation and born in 1971, writes:

> Television, movies, and school programs have told us we were special from toddlerhood to high school, and we believe it with a self-confidence that approaches boredom: why talk about it? It's just the way things are. This blasé attitude is very different from the Boomer focus on introspection and self-absorption: GenMe is not self-absorbed; we're self-important. We take it for granted that we're independent, special individuals, so we don't really need to think about it.[2]

Although the label of "entitled" may be regularly branded on today's Millennials or Gen Ys, my experience tells a different story. All generations can boast examples of the "me first" crowd. After all, attitudes and behaviors are contagious. When respect for others became a notion that was passé, it wasn't just one generation that suffered. All generations have members more than willing to shift their attention from others and focus it on themselves. As a result, civility suffers, and so does our society.

The partner of self-entitlement is lack of appreciation. Favors are expected of others and when people grant them, there's not a hint of thanks. One manager told me of trying to regularly help direct reports by covering for them on holidays and providing better schedules for them at her own expense. Rather than ever receiving a word of thanks from the employees, what should have been appreciation became expectation. When she no longer was in a position to cover for them, the employees were in shock that they'd have to carry their own weight.

Entitlement isn't limited to the workplace. Thank you notes for wedding gifts and birthday presents are increasingly the exception rather than the rule. RSVPs are left lingering as hosts of events wonder whether they're going to feed one hungry guest or a crowd. People regularly complain that invited guests wait until the very last minute to RSVP in case a better offer shows up. The sense of entitlement in the personal life transitions into the professional life.

If we approach work with the idea that we're entitled to be treated with special favors, fewer responsibilities, and with moving deadlines, the outcome will be behavior that comes off as self-entitled. Self-entitlement does not prompt civility. As with anything in your diet that doesn't contribute to your healthier lifestyle, it needs to be tossed out. The sense of self-entitlement is no better for your civil self than is a great big hot fudge sundae to your waistline—no matter how much you feel you deserve it.

Rumination

You've made a mistake, and now you can't stop thinking about. It happened this morning, and you're still chewing over what you should have done differently.

You asked your colleague to switch schedules with you so that you could attend your daughter's recital, and she barked at you that you always wait until the last minute to ask favors. She firmly replied, "no!" For the rest of the day you dwell on her response, her body language, and her tone of voice. You can't let it go, and in fact, are struggling not to let her have it in the middle of the office.

You ruminate! *Ruminate* is defined by Merriam Webster as "to go over in the mind repeatedly and often casually or slowly."[3] Rumination shows up when something negative occurs, and we rehearse the episode over and over again. That thought process drains us and sets us up to react from a negative vantage point out of self-pity, anger, or self-righteousness. Just like cleaning out your kitchen cabinets of anything that will sabotage your diet, rumination needs to be cleared from your pantry of emotional staples.

If you tend to ruminate, knock it off! It's getting in the way of your civil self. Instead, realize you learned from your mistake or that of another, and maintain your civil self.

Authenticity

The demand for authenticity is a constant refrain. We all want the real deal—not something that's fake, a fraud, or inauthentic. However, when it comes to behavior, authenticity can be used as an excuse for rudeness, and a vehicle for emotional discharge in the workplace.

Civility is not about being fake. It *is* about thoughtfulness and consideration for others. Just because you feel queasy after last night's dinner at the in-laws, authenticity doesn't require a detailed description to a colleague's greeting asking how you're doing. That person you work with is trying to connect, not diagnose what's currently ailing you.

Being authentic does not let you off the hook when it comes to courtesy. Consistent implementation of respect for the other guy or gal doesn't mean you get to pick and choose the moments when you're in the mood to be gracious. Systematic civility is like a systematic approach to exercise. As Nike so eloquently says, "Just do it!"

Quoting Dr. Michael Yapko in his book *Depression is Contagious*:

> Some people justify their negativity—their constant complaints, cynical comments, or criticism—by saying, "Well, it's how I feel. It would be phony to act like everything's okay when it isn't." Do you think it's generally more important to be honest or to be easy to get along with? Under what specific conditions do you think it's more important to be pleasant than authentic? And under what conditions would you say the opposite is true?

> There is an important distinction between honesty and discretion. You don't have to say everything you think or share everything you feel. There are situations in which it is more important to get along (avoid unnecessary conflict) than it is to be honest. That's true in families and it's true in the business world.[4]

Authenticity is to be applauded as long as it's not an excuse for uncivil behavior. If you're using it for justification to be disrespectful, dump authenticity along with the chips and soda.

Unhealthy Choices

Lack of sleep, poor nutrition, and no exercise are all superlative ingredients to create an uncivil self.

When you and I don't get enough sleep, we're grumpy, impatient, and hard to please! (I admit it—my family steers clear of me when I'm short on sleep!) As if crankiness isn't bad enough, lack of sleep can lead to our inability to catch on quickly, to concentrate, and to problem solve. Now your colleagues and superiors are dealing with someone who's a curmudgeon *and* isn't performing well!

Eating too much junk and too little protein and veggies takes a toll on our health. Our energy dwindles, and when that happens we're less resilient and less able to deal with stress. And you know where that leads—to incivility!

Our bodies crave exercise—it releases hormones. Michael Otto, a professor of psychology at Boston University says, "The link between exercise and mood is pretty strong. Usually within five minutes of moderate exercise, you get a mood-enhancement effect."[5]

That mood-enhancement effect better positions us to deal with stress and to remain our civil self.

So as you look at your list of what has to go, here are three suggestions:

- **Lack of sleep.** If you're waking up exhausted from too little sleep, try getting to sleep just one hour earlier at night. Consider cutting back on your social media and television hours at night. You just might regain an hour or two for some much needed shut-eye.

- **Junk food.** A healthier diet fuels your civil self. Remember, garbage in, garbage out.

- **Too little exercise.** Pull out the calendar and carve out time for you and your exercise of choice. Get that civil self of yours up and moving!

There's yet another unhealthy choice that we too often make for all the wrong reasons. Out of the desire for attention, the appearance of knowing inside information, or the ugly goal of stirring the pot, we gossip! We've all been guilty of gossiping about the business, our leadership, colleagues, or customers. It's never for a good reason and never has good results. In his bestseller, *EntreLeadership*, financial guru Dave Ramsey says: "Gossip about the company, or about leadership, is a particularly evil form of disloyalty. And it is suicidal when the person gossiping is hurting and running down the place and the people who pay him so he can feed his family."[6] Ramsey's policy on gossip is simple: no gossip allowed. If you're caught gossiping you get one warning. Then you're out!

Eliminating gossip is a choice that will not only lead to a more civil you, but a far healthier environment.

Garbage Collection

So what fills your mind? Is it the life lessons learned from countless hours of reality TV or video games?

With whom do you hang out? People who bring out the best in you, or people who leave you in a worse emotional place than when you joined them?

How do you fill your time away from work? Enjoying outdoor sports with friends, stimulating conversations with family, taking a fabulous course on a subject brand new to you? Perhaps, it's spending hours posting on social media or watching marathon episodes of the latest vampire series?

How you answer those questions is instructive as to whether your influences are putting you into an easier or more difficult position to achieve and maintain your civil self. Like any diet, what and how we feed ourselves is critical to our success in achieving good health. Our minds are no different. Our intake of intellectual and emotional ingredients nurtures either civility or incivility. We're not only creatures of habit, but creatures of influence.

Television and movies influence our choices in style, language, and behavior. Research indicates that the catty, nasty behavior of reality TV may be a poor influence on our own reality.[7] Writing for *The Huffington Post*, Dr. Gail Gross cautions, "Studies show that violence on television does have an adverse effect on children and the way they think and act. This is true not only for young children, but some recent studies indicate that watching violence on television can even impact adults."[8]

Strategic planning shouldn't be a phrase restricted to the workplace. **We need to strategically plan what goes into our mind!**

When we're surrounded by people who are crude, crass, and cranky, their behavior rubs off onto us. It's not long before our language takes a toll, our thoughtfulness dims, and our joy is usurped. We quickly become a negative influence personally and professionally. Our civil self is a goner!

Whatever is influencing us to be less than our best, dump it! That includes people. I know that sounds harsh, but if your friends aren't a positive and uplifting influence, then it's time to find friends who are. What you watch, what you read, what you hear—they all need to make up a healthy menu of influences that propel you toward your civil self.

No Systems in Place

Life is always easier with a system! In the workplace, when we don't get things done accurately and on time, it's usually because we don't have a system in place.

A diet is nothing more than a system of eating. A workout plan is a system of exercising. A system forces us to do something in an expected pattern, a routine. Systematizing an endeavor makes it predictable, simpler, and repeatable.

When we dumped manners, we actually tossed out a systematic approach to civility. Manners were a system that was predictable, simple, and repeatable. Without a foundation of manners, we're left with a workforce struggling to understand that *please, thank you,* and *you're welcome* convey verbal respect for the customer and for one another.

Let me give you an idea of how a systematic approach via manners used to work at home and in the workplace.

1. When you requested something, you said *please.*
2. When someone gave you something or did something thoughtful for you, you said *thank you.*
3. When someone responded thank you, you answered, *you're welcome.* (It was far superior to *yup, uh huh,* or a grunt and nod.)
4. When you passed through a doorway, you held the door open for people coming in either direction. It's thoughtful.
5. You were expected to have a working knowledge of vocabulary without the regular dependence on expletives, obscenities, F-bombs, or #&!s.

6. Phone conversations were between you and the person on the other end of the phone. They were not shared (or blared) to everyone within a football field of proximity.

This systematic approach to civility did something very important. It made us aware of others so that we didn't take them or their actions for granted. Is it perfect? Of course not! But what a great place to start! Emily Post might have described manners as a system that demonstrates, "a sensitive awareness of the feelings of others."[9]

Pier M. Forni, professor of Italian literature at John Hopkins University and author of *Choosing Civility* says, "Good manners are the training wheels of altruism."[10]

Time to begin systematizing your civility—it starts with manners.

Ignorance

Research shows that up and down the business ladder, people don't know what civility is. Quoting again from *Generation Me*, Jean Twenge writes,

> Not caring what others think may also explain the decline in manners and politeness. Because we no longer believe that there is one right way of doing things, most of us were never taught the rules of etiquette. Although it's fine to wear white shoes after Labor Day and use whatever fork you want, most etiquette was developed to provide something often lacking in modern life: respect for other people's comfort.[11]

OK, a little explanation might be needed here. When I was a little girl, fashion dictated that no one, especially anyone living in a big metropolitan city, should wear white shoes after Labor Day. It should be obvious that that was about fashion trends, not the respect for other people's comfort.

The respect for the well-being of others is at the heart of manners. When parents taught their children to stand up and offer their seat to the elderly person or the pregnant woman who had no place to sit on the crowded bus or in the standing-room only area, it taught youngsters to value others of different generations or in different stages of life.

If you don't know how to be civil, dump the excuse of "ignorance"—and keep reading.

Out They Go!

You're serious about your civil self, and in an endeavor to make civility stronger and more flexible, you've committed to excluding these eight obstacles to become your best civil self:

- Excuses
- Entitlement
- Rumination
- Authenticity
- Unhealthy Choices
- Our Personal Intake of Garbage
- No Systems in Place
- Ignorance

In the next chapter, we're going to talk about what to replace all the mental rubbish with. But first, let's review how you're going to exercise your civil self by working the **Civility Wrap-up**; then we're off to **C's the Day!**

Civility Wrap-Up

- Civility comes from within.
- To be civil to others, we must first be civil to ourselves.
- We have to practice being our best civil selves.
- Civility is a matter of conscious choice.
- Eliminate these eight things from your civil self diet:
  - Excuses
  - Entitlement
  - Rumination
  - Authenticity
  - Unhealthy Choices
  - Our Personal Intake of Garbage
  - No Systems in Place
  - Ignorance

C's the Day

Please review your score from the Civility Quotient Assessment you took earlier in the chapter (and if you didn't, please take a few moments now to complete it). Give yourself a pat on the back for the items you've mastered! Now, identify five areas where you need to improve (think something you scored as 3 or lower). Write down one thing you can do consistently each day to improve in these five areas. Remember, practice makes the civil self!

Communicating Character by Exercising Civility

NOTES CHAPTER 11

1   Jim Collins, *Good to Great: Why Some Companies Make the Leap...and Others Don't* (New York: HarperBusiness, 2011), 11.

2   Jean M. Twenge, *Generation Me: Why Today's Young Americans Are More Confident, Assertive, Entitled—and More Miserable Than Ever Before* (New York: Atria, 2006), 4.

3   Merriam-Webster's Collegiate Dictionary, 11th ed., s.v. "ruminate."

4   Michael D. Yapko, *Depression Is Contagious: How the Most Common Mood Disorder Is Spreading around the World and How to Stop It* (New York: Free Press, 2009), 97.

5   Kirsten Weir, "The Exercise Effect," *Monitor on Psychology* 42, no. 11 (December 2011), www.apa.org/monitor/2011/12/exercise.aspx.

6   Dave Ramsey, *EntreLeadership: 20 Years of Practical Business Wisdom from the Trenches* (New York: Howard Books, 2011), 233.

7   Philip Ross, "Reality TV's Impact on Viewers: How Shows Like 'The Real Housewives' and 'The Hills' Affect Perceptions of What's Normal," *International Science Times*, September 16, 2013, www.isciencetimes.com/articles/6069/20130916/reality-tv-s-impact-viewers-shows-real.htm.

8   Gail Gross, "Violence on TV and How It Can Affect Your Children," *Huffington Post*, August 15, 2013 updated October 15, 2013, www.huffingtonpost.com/dr-gail-gross/violence-on-tv-children_b_3734764.html.

9   Peggy Post, Anna Post, Lizzie Post, and Daniel Post Senning, *Emily Post's Etiquette: Manners for a New World*, 18th ed. (New York: HarperCollins, 2011).

10 Alina Tugend, "Incivility Can Have Costs Beyond Hurt Feelings," *New York Times*, November 9, 2010, www.nytimes.com/2010/11/20/your-money/20shortcuts.html.

11 Jean M. Twenge, *Generation Me: Why Today's Young Americans Are More Confident, Assertive, Entitled—and More Miserable Than Ever Before* (New York: Atria, 2006), 26.

CHAPTER 12
The Civil Self Success Plan

We all know the secret to a successful health program—work! It's exactly the same with The Civility Workout—work, discipline, and healthy choices. Making the commitment to regularly exercise civility becomes a habit that changes you and your life, both personally and professionally.

Civility truly changes lives. We know that emotions and behaviors are contagious. Our civil behavior and consistent implementation of respect for others generate a change that creates an environment that is healthy, strong, and promotes superior outcomes.

In the last chapter, I asked you to eliminate several things from your daily routine—"diet" if you will. Now, it's time to replace those bad habits with the following eight positive ones, which will leave you feeling full—full of positivity and wholeness:

- Attention
- Boundaries
- Humor
- Perception
- Healthy Choices
- Consistency
- Smile
- The Best Choice Ever

Attention

Recently, I nearly hit a teenager! In the middle of a block, no crosswalk or pedestrian marking in sight, this teenager and his friend sauntered in front of my car as I drove down the street. They never so much as glanced in my direction. I slammed on my brakes and honked to get their attention. I was greeted with a lovely middle finger, a look of contempt, and a very loud "f*** you!" Staring at their phones and buried in conversation, the duo paid no attention to anything taking place around them.

If the unaware pedestrian is an unknown experience for you, perhaps my next example will seem more familiar. You're shopping in a warehouse store when you see a crowd huddled around a diminutive figure looking down. As the gathering of people seems stuck and unable to move aside for fellow shoppers, you assume the worst. Their attention must be focused on some emergency, someone who needs help.

Nope...they're bunched around a sampling of food, totally unaware of the traffic jam they've created by their refusal to move until sufficiently stuffed with bites of hors d'oeuvres and desserts.

Attention to others—*their* needs and *their* emotions—is absolutely essential to cultivate and develop our civil self. Pivoting our focus from ourselves to others begins to open our hearts and minds to the generating of respect for other human beings. The attention we bring to our moments with others begins to instruct us as to how to strengthen our civil self.

Boundaries

"Good fences make good neighbors." The quote, attributed to poet Robert Frost, may appear contradictory; however, it succinctly states the importance of knowing our boundaries in any relationship, be it professional, personal, or our relationship with ourselves.

Boundaries are teaching tools. They educate people as to what behaviors are acceptable to you. When you set clear boundaries, and respectfully forbid someone to push or overstep those boundaries, you're telling them, "this far and no further."

Too often we permit people to treat us disrespectfully, but don't say a word to them. As far as they're concerned, their behavior is acceptable. After all, we accepted their treatment of us without saying a word.

In chapter 3, I mentioned that when someone publicly humiliates you, your choices aren't limited to either accepting humiliation or letting the jerk have it. There is a third choice—set your boundaries. Make it very clear that public reprimands are unacceptable. In other words, don't keep quiet. After the incident, take the time to collect yourself. This may be a matter of minutes, hours, or even a full day. Physically, breathe! Cool down so that you can think clearly. With confidence (even if you have to fake it), set up a time to see that individual. Spell out to them that raising their voice at you and rebuking you in public is unacceptable. Neither be apologetic in approach nor lambast the person. This isn't about getting even, it's about getting clarity. It can be helpful to be empathetic and explain that you understand the stress and pressure they (the offender) felt at that moment. But remember—that doesn't give them license to be a jerk. Explain exactly the respectful behavior that you'd like to see. Although there's no 100 percent guarantee that this will eliminate future episodes, you can feel confident that you have made it clear what you consider acceptable and what is not.

Whether it's interrupting, asking too personal of questions, trying to engage you in gossip, or just ignoring your emails requesting much needed information, unless you define your boundaries, people will maintain their same behavior toward you. In fact, they may even push it.

My husband and I had been married a couple of years when one evening, the fences went up...clearly and powerfully. I was perpetually late—late to everything, even work! One night as we headed over to some friends for dinner, late as usual, I began to apologize for my tardiness. This, by the way, was standard operating procedure. Leave the house late, apologize, leave late, apologize, leave late—it was an ugly cycle. Until that night, I'd not only pushed the boundaries, I had totally ignored any sense of courtesy for my husband or our hosts. So there I was right in the middle of apologies when my husband responded, "No, you're not sorry. If you were sorry, you wouldn't be late. Obviously, you think that your time is more important than anyone else's." The fence was set. It wasn't moving. I couldn't push, pull, or jump over it. The only response that was respectful was to be punctual. And today, with very rare exceptions, I am. My husband set the boundary, and I learned a well-needed lesson in respecting others and their time.

Boundaries are the way we teach others how to treat us. The boundaries of others are, also, our guides as to how to treat them with respect. Boundaries are vital for the civil self.

Humor

Lighten up! As a society, we have lost our ability to laugh at ourselves.

One of my greatest joys is to have worked with people who are ferociously serious about their work, but not about themselves. As Tom Peters says in his book *The Pursuit of WOW*:

> Lighten up. I despise stuffed shirts! It's pure prejudice, I know, but I like and trust people who put their feet up, spout an occasional four-letter word, and laugh at their *own screw-ups*."[1]

I agree with Peters. I've worked with magnificent people who do magnificent work and can laugh at themselves and laugh with others. I've also worked with people who do magnificent work, but who can't discover laughter, light-heartedness, or fun in any part of their job. It's humor that mitigates stress, resets an ugly moment, and allows us to consider our own ability to make mistakes and survive.

Viktor Frankl, Austrian neurologist, psychiatrist, and holocaust survivor, said, "I never would have made it if I could not have laughed. It lifted me momentarily out of this horrible situation, just enough to make it livable."[2]

Laughter breaks the spell of negativity, criticism, and even incivility. Humor is one of the key ingredients you and I need to strengthen our civil selves.

Perspective

The Roman emperor Marcus Aurelius is quoted as saying, "Everything we hear is an opinion, not a fact. Everything we see is a perspective, not the truth."[3]

If you ask five colleagues about the meeting they all just attended together, it's likely you'll hear five different descriptions of what happened in that meeting. They were all in the same room, heard the same words, and received the same printed agenda. They listened to the same speakers and watched the exact same presentations, but their life experiences, both in and out of the workplace, painted their observations with entirely different shades, textures, and intensity. Each has a different opinion and perspective of what transpired.

Our ability to step into the shoes of someone else and begin to understand their perspective fuels our ability to engage with others through the civil self. Why is it so difficult for us to try to understand the other person's viewpoint? It takes humility!

In my coaching of leadership teams, I'm always struck by how easily individuals get locked into their own viewpoint, their own opinion, and their own definition of how to conduct business effectively. For many, shifting from their own personal viewpoint and adjusting for the viewpoints of others is not easy. Yet until team members begin to peek through the lenses of their fellow colleagues and look at the issues from those newly gained perspectives, it's extraordinarily difficult to unleash civility in the environment.

Understanding another's perspective not only makes exercising civility more fun, it makes it more successful.

Healthy Choices

The potato chips or the broccoli? The second helping of meat and potatoes, or one moderate portion of each? An afternoon of couch sitting and TV watching or a brisk three-mile walk? With each option, we have to make a choice. Although one choice may be more fun and delicious for the moment, the other option will lead to healthier long-term results.

Is it easy? Usually, no, at least not until it becomes a habit. Will you get better results? Yes. You and I are constantly in the position of making healthy choices.

Too often we read of Hollywood stars who seem to have everything you could possibly want in life: family, friends, buckets of money, and influence. Yet, consistently they make poor choices. As a result, sponsors, producers, and cast members become nervous. Choices of booze, late nights, and partying continue to put schedules and expectations at risk. Dependability is uncertain.

When you and I make poor choices, it affects not just us, but those around us. When I was constantly late, my husband was stressed and annoyed, hosts were irritated, and dinners were cold. Even our safety was at risk as we looked at speed limits as suggestions and yellow traffic signals as bright colored lights to beckon us on.

Sometimes our continued poor choices force others to make unpleasant choices on our behalf. Choose to show up late at work repeatedly, and a choice will be made for you: you're fired.

Everything about our civil self involves choice: The choice to put ourselves into a healthier position through our choices of diet and exercise. The choice to exercise civility through patience and respectful behavior. The choice to perform as promised.

The civil self works to consistently make healthy choices that promote, and yes, even protect our civility.

Consistency

The key to civility is consistency! Consistent behavior, consistent performance, consistent communication. Nothing kills civility like inconsistency.

We've all worked for the boss who is all sunshine one day and thunderbolts the next. You never know what to expect when you walk in the door. You hope for the best, yet you prepare for the worst. But it's not just inconsistent behavior that sets up fertile ground for incivility to arise from stress and frustration. Inconsistent messaging can wreak havoc.

Leaders, too often, are inconsistent with their instructions. They tell some people one way of doing something and other people another way of doing the same thing. Directives change not only from person to person, but from day to day. Goals that are agreed upon, set, and communicated frequently change in what seems like a matter of moments. People are left frustrated, angry, and stressed out. When people feel they've wasted time and effort, emotions that fuel incivility can quickly arise!

Promises made and not kept, whether it's a scheduled delivery of product to a customer or a scheduled delivery of necessary paperwork to a colleague, are the perfect ingredients for incivility to erupt. At the heart of each example is inconsistency.

More than 2,000 years ago, the Greek philosopher Epictetus told us how to prevent such inconsistency: "First say to yourself what you would be; and then do what you have to do."

One of the great enemies of consistency is emotion. In fact, Coach John Wooden says that emotion is your enemy. According to Wooden:

> Good judgment, common sense, and reason all fly out the window when emotions kick down your door. Unfortunately, this usually happens in times of turmoil or crisis when you and your organization can least afford it.[4]

> Emotionalism—ups and downs in moods, displays of temperament—is almost always counterproductive, and at times disastrous. I came to understand that if my own behavior was filled with emotionalism, I was sanctioning it for others.[5]

> My teaching stressed that "losing your temper will get us outplayed because you'll make unnecessary errors; your judgment will be impaired." I didn't mind an occasional mistake unless it was caused by loss of self-control.[6]

Another example of inconsistency that drives the wedge of incivility between a company and its customers, between teams and staff, and within an organization is inconsistent communication! In today's world of 24/7 technology, unanswered questions, poorly worded messaging, and error-laden writing conspire quickly to take down respectful behavior within organizations. If people are waiting on you to respond in order to be able to take the next step, your incivility is sowing the seeds of distrust and disrespect by severing links to civil communication and your highest sense of character.

Consistency in actions, performance, and communication generate positive emotions of predictability, dependability, and integrity. In your civil self diet, always reach for consistency.

Smile

"We shall never know all the good that a simple smile can do."[7] Mother Teresa's words always make me smile. Researchers tell us that the mere act of smiling is better than a prescription for hormones. Psychologists claim that if we smile, we might turn around race relations.[8] Beauty experts advise that if we would just smile, we'd drop ten years. A smile is our own personal weapon to persuade, calm, and connect. And it should come naturally. We start smiling when we're in the womb![9]

Professor Stuart Campbell, an English obstetrician who began the use of a 4D scanner to monitor babies in the womb says that once a baby makes his or her entrance into the world, they normally don't smile until they're six weeks old. However, images captured by the 4D scanner show that babies smile, cry, and blink before birth. Referring to babies' pre-birth smiles, Professor Campbell says, "What's behind the smile, of course, I can't say, but the corners turn up and the cheeks bulge...I think it must be some indication of contentment in a stress-free environment."[10]

Out of the womb, all grown up, and working in anything but a stress-free environment, our smiles are in short supply. Yet, it's our smile that permeates our surroundings and sends out emotional signals and triggers.

Smiles also affect behavior. According to Daniel McNeill, author of *The Face: A Natural History,* while "courtroom judges are equally likely to find smilers and non-smilers guilty, they give smilers lighter penalties, a phenomenon called the 'smile-leniency effect.'"[11]

Smiling is a vital part of any language, especially the language of business. However, unlike learning conjugations and vocabulary, we just need to learn to lighten up and smile. Your smile is invaluable because it's contagious. I challenge you to go through the day and smile. Smile at your colleagues whether peer, direct report, or supervisor. The dividends are immense. If nothing else, it will keep them guessing!

Your smile is absolutely essential to your civil self!

The Best Choice Ever

Do you know how you can make the lives of everyone around you better and easier? All you have to do is to make one choice. It's not a difficult choice, but it's also not a popular choice. You *will* be in the minority; however, you will also be in huge demand. People will want to work with you, be with you, connect with you. It's one simple choice...and here it is: Choose not to be offended!

That's it. It's a simple choice, but I grant one that's not always easy. These days we quickly take offense to what people say and what people do and what people don't say or what people don't do. I'm asking you to make the choice to *not* take offense!

When you and I tell another person that we're offended by some comment, we have just made ourselves the victim and them the villain. You don't have to *like* what the other person says or does, but choosing to take offense sets up a situation that either shuts down conversation immediately or escalates it to ugly. Making the choice to not take offense puts you in a better position to maintain civility...at least toward yourself.

Exercise the choice to not take offense!

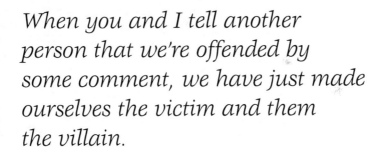

When you and I tell another person that we're offended by some comment, we have just made ourselves the victim and them the villain.

YOU ARE JUDGED BY THE COMPANY YOU KEEP

One of the best ways to succeed in The Civility Workout is by choosing the right people with whom to surround yourself. I give you the guidance from a woman and a man who have had tremendous influences on the lives of others:

Oprah Winfrey's recommendation is simple, "Surround yourself with only people who are going to lift you higher."[12] These are the people who switch on your energy, bring a smile to your face, and inspire you to be even better. However, these are also the people who will challenge you and not let you sell yourself short. They demand more of you.

Coach John Wooden said, "I believe that you must have people around you willing to ask questions and express opinions, people who seek improvement for the organization rather than merely gaining favor with the boss. Look for these people when hiring and making promotion decisions."[13] It may be tempting to surround yourself with those who agree with your every move, but resist. The person who argues with you may see possibilities in you that you just don't see. They may be just the influence you need!

As we demand better influences, we create better habits. When you surround yourself with people who exercise regularly, eat healthy, and make great choices, you begin to learn to make their healthy habits your healthy habits. And when you surround yourself with people who exercise civility regularly and make great choices, you begin to learn to make their habits of how to treat people your own habits of civility.

All civility begins with you: making the commitment, taking the steps, and following through with The Civility Workout. As you make it part of your daily life—a habit—you'll find that you have become stronger, more flexible, and with a heart full of wisdom.

Here you go...please review the **Civility Wrap-up**, and then **C's the Day**!

Civility Wrap-Up

■ There are eight keys to successfully implementing The Civil Self Success Plan:

- Attention

- Boundaries

- Humor

- Perception

- Healthy Choices

- Consistency

- Smile

- The Best Choice Ever

C's the Day

Please review the eight items in this chapter. What is the easiest item on the list for you to implement? What's the most difficult? If you want to make changes in your civil self, start by making little changes that are easier for you to achieve. Little changes reap big rewards, especially when done consistently. Once you make those a habit, try to tackle a bigger challenge. You might just find you like it!

Communicating Character by Exercising Civility

NOTES CHAPTER 12

1 Tom Peters, *The Pursuit of WOW!* (New York: Vintage Books, 1994), 7 (emphasis added).

2 Viktor E. Frankl, *Man's Search for Meaning* (Cutchogue, NY: Buccaneer Books, 1959).

3 Marcus Aurelius, BrainyQuote.com, Xplore Inc. (2015), www.brainyquote.com/quotes/quotes/m/marcusaure143088.html.

4 John Wooden and Steve Jamison, *Wooden on Leadership* (New York: McGraw-Hill, 2005), 108.

5 Ibid., 112.

6 Ibid., 113.

7 Mother Teresa, BrainyQuote.com, Xplore Inc. (2015), www.brainyquote.com/quotes/quotes/m/mothertere125711.html.

8 Richard Manly, "Go Ahead and Smile," http://web.csulb.edu/misc/inside/archives/v59n1/1.htm.

9 "Babies Smile in the Womb," www.dailymail.co.uk/health/article-196020/Babies-smile-womb.html.

10 Ibid.

11 Dale Carnegie & Associates, *How to Win Friends & Influence People in the Digital Age* (New York: Simon & Schuster, 2011), 52.

12 Oprah Winfrey, BrainyQuote.com, Xplore Inc. (2015), www.brainyquote.com/quotes/quotes/o/oprahwinfr383697.html.

13 John Wooden and Steve Jamison, *Wooden on Leadership* (New York: McGraw-Hill, 2005), 202.

CHAPTER 13
Protecting Yourself When You're Incivility's Target

If you are caught up in a toxic environment right now, please know that my heart goes out to you. I have an idea that any of the following may be what you're feeling and what's going through your head:

I dread going to work. I can't do anything right. I don't trust anyone anymore. It seems like no one cares, and I used to have a great relationship with the staff. I'm afraid that if I make one mistake, I'm out the door. I need the job; I'm letting my family down. If I go to HR, it will get back to my boss. I'm afraid that I'm going to burst into tears at any moment. I can't sleep. I can't eat. I can't do anything right! I'm tired all the time. I can't even think straight anymore. I feel like my friends and family hate to see me coming—I'm always so down. **I can't do anything right!** *I used to love this profession—now I just want to get out. Why can't I turn things around? What is happening? Am I going crazy?*

If you are fortunate enough never to have been ensnared in a toxic environment, you may think that I'm exaggerating or being overly dramatic. Not for a moment! From my own experience and from speaking with men and women of all ages and nationalities from countless industries, any or all of these emotions are exactly what you may be feeling. Although this book focuses on the necessity to exercise civility toward others, it's imperative that you start with yourself—especially if you're in a toxic environment. You must exercise civility toward you! It's important to be kind, generous, and honest with yourself. However, this does not mean excusing your own poor behavior.

My respect for you coupled with your own self-respect demand your being accountable to yourself. Begin by reviewing your Civility Quotient

Assessment to determine whether you are, in fact, exercising civility toward others, especially anyone who seems to be targeting for you. Is it possible that their rudeness, undermining, gossip, or intentional miscommunication is a response to your own poor behavior? Could it be that another's cold and unkind interactions with you is the result of your own thoughtlessness? Granted, there are people who love to use power to create drama, but even in the most toxic of circumstances it's crucial to begin with you! Assess objectively whether it's possible that you failed to consistently exercise civility. When going through your assessment, it's critical that you don't draw conclusions based on a feeling of guilt within yourself or your desire to assign guilt to others. Try to step back and act as an observer of your own conduct. Don't focus on those one or two interactions that went poorly or the one or two that went well. Try to observe your typical, consistent behavior.

If negativity has become your normal mode of thinking, you may want to review your assessment with a colleague whom you thoroughly trust to determine your Civility Quotient.

If your assessment shows that you regularly employ civility and yet you find that someone still has it out for you, it's time to turn the focus to what you can do to protect yourself while stuck in this mess.

IS YOUR NEGATIVE SELF-TALK ACCURATE?

Before I walk through the steps to help protect you as you navigate the land mines of a toxic environment, please let me provide a bit of perspective on that dismal self-talk I referred to earlier.

I dread going to work. Believe me, I know—but let's see how we can turn that around. You cannot change the people at work, especially whoever your tormenter is, but you can change your attitude and your behavior. I know it seems impossible, and I'm not playing Pollyanna, but if you have to go to work, you must position yourself better. If you wake up dwelling on everything that can go wrong and everything that has gone wrong, you will never move forward.

I don't trust anyone anymore. Sure you do. You trust yourself. Trust that you are better than this experience. Trust that you will learn from this ordeal and come out of it stronger, smarter, and with a ton more self-respect.

It seems like no one cares, and I used to have a great relationship with the staff. People do care, you just don't know who. In a toxic environment, fear takes prisoners of those with best intentions. In fear of retribution or losing their jobs, people withhold their camaraderie and often their compassion. This is where your humanity plays a huge role—forgive them. It's not about you or them—it's about fear.

I'm afraid that if I make one mistake, I'm out the door. Honestly, that is possible. And that is exactly why remaining confident and taking these steps to strengthen yourself are so important. Under the mantle of anxiety and panic, you won't do your best work.

I need the job; I'm letting my family down. I'm not going to tell you to quit and find a new job. I'm going to tell you to, again, pivot your focus. You may need your current job, at least for now, but framing the situation in terms of dire and drastic will reduce your confidence and your ability to take control. See this as an opportunity to learn absolutely everything you can at the company's expense.

If I go to HR, it will get back to my boss...and the problem is my boss! Yes, there's a chance that your boss will hear about your visit to HR. While you make your determination about visiting HR, consider this: the best way to eradicate something that's toxic and harmful is to shine the light on it. If abusive behavior remains in the dark, it will also remain very much alive and destructive. Think about a possible mentor or supervisor who may have the experience you need to help you make this decision.

I'm afraid I'll burst into tears any moment. You may be framing yourself as the victim, and that's keeping you on edge. As long as you see yourself as the victim, you'll remain on the verge of tears. Once you're in the privacy of your own home, go ahead and have that cry and get it out of your system...but then move on and confront yourself with why you see yourself as a victim.

I can't sleep. I can't eat. I can't do anything right. I'm tired all the time. I can't even think straight anymore. I bet you haven't made time for exercise. Exercise will help rid you of the stress, build your appetite, and generate your energy. When you're exhausted and eating poorly, it's more difficult to think clearly and easier to make mistakes.

I used to love this profession—now I just want to get out. Why can't I turn things around? What is happening? Am I going crazy? Don't worry, you're not alone...and no, you're not going crazy. However, too many of our workplaces have us tied up in knots. Out of ignorance or with full intention, there are bosses, supervisors, and colleagues who wreak havoc. You may not be able to turn around the workplace, but you can change your response to it...and it's important that you do!

CHANGE YOUR PERSPECTIVE AND PROCESS

I know what you're thinking or yelling at the book (and to me) right now! "What do you know? I am a victim. I've done my very best, and now I've being treated like I'm (fill in the blank): worthless, incompetent, a short-timer, invisible, not a human being." I guarantee that as long as you see yourself as a victim, you won't be able to move forward and out of that feeling of helplessness. When all those corrosive thoughts start tromping through your brain, take action immediately. Do not let them get the upper hand. You're stuck, but you're definitely not finished. Let's walk through this together so that you can truly **C's the Day**, and stop letting all that vile behavior seize you.

Step One: Focus First

First thing in the morning, open your eyes and focus on something wonderful. It may be that your favorite team won the playoffs, that your child was tapped for a part in the school play, or that someone you cherish is right next to you. Be thankful for the mere fact that you woke up at all! Look outside: nature always has gifts that we don't take time to appreciate. Turning immediately to prayer or meditation turns on appreciation and turns off resentment for many people. Deciding to go for a run and thinking about today's goals could be what gets your blood flowing and stops the ruminating.

Step Two: Follow-through from the Beginning

Create a morning routine that sets you in the right mood for the day and gets your body going in the right direction. For me, it's prayer, exercise, and breakfast. I get out of bed prepared to take those three steps. I may change the sequence around, but my routine is predictable and primes me emotionally, spiritually, and physically. What's your sequence?

Step Three: Interact with Others in Mind

Commit to a change in attitude. You must steer yourself from negative to positive. You don't have to be a motivational speaker first thing in the morning to everyone at home, but you owe it to those around you to be pleasant and positive. You affect the start of their day as well.

Step Four: Express Yourself

Smile. I don't care whether you feel like it—just smile already! Remember, it changes you physically. You don't have to even mean it—just do it! Right now...come on...smile!

Step Five: Be Your Own Choreographer

Play music! There's a reason that we exercise to music; it makes all that work a lot easier and more fun. Olympic gold medalist swimmer Michael Phelps is known for listening to music in preparation for competition. Phelps says that Lil Wayne's "Right Above It," "made me want to finish strong and look forward to life after swimming."[1] If an Olympic athlete uses music as a performance enhancement tool, doesn't it make sense that you and I should, too?

Listening to music first thing at home before you head out the door, in the car as you drive into work, at lunch and on breaks, and as you head home can cut right through dark feelings and lift your spirits.

Step Six: Pull Out the Mirror

Ladies and gentlemen, dress to look your very best. Be sure you pull out what fits you well (that may prompt a new diet and exercise program). Now pay close attention to what you see in the mirror. Is your clothing clean? Is it accessorized well? Is it appropriate for the workplace?

Are buttons buttoned, zippers zipped, and is anything showing that shouldn't? Your work environment is the last place you need a wardrobe malfunction.

Step Seven: Make an Entrance

Change your entrance. Walk into work like you own it. I mean it. Stand up tall. Chin up, head up, shoulders back. Don't think I'm being superficial. There's a reason that actors spend countless hours mastering the physical presence of their characters. Everything we see about the character sends a message to us about that role. Don't walk in like your work owns you, walk in like you own your work!

Step Eight: Take Notes

If day-in and day-out you're dealing with the rude, destructive, and caustic behavior of a supervisor, boss, or colleague, take notes. I hate the idea of heading down this path, but we're talking real world application. If someone doesn't take action to clean up the environment, you know as well as I do that legal action could be in the future. Taking notes not only puts you in a better position to defend yourself, but substantiates that you are not going crazy—those absurd interactions truly took place. (By the way, notes are for the boss as well. Too often that toxic employee stays too long and does too much damage because supervisors fail to take the time to chronicle the employee's disruptive and detrimental behavior.)

Step Nine: Create a New Commentary

Cancel the old and create the new commentary. Have you ever noticed that we go through the day with a running commentary playing in our brains? That non-stop narration may be one negative critical message after another about other people, what's happening at the moment, and about ourselves. Picture yourself clicking off that old negative messaging, and click on the new. Create new descriptions and explanations that take you to a new and powerful place.

Step Ten: Change the Scenery

It's important that you don't see yourself as a helpless victim inside your workplace. Take your breaks, take a walk, and take some music. It may sound cliché, but physical changes help to reframe the situation.

Challenge yourself! Change your mind, change your self-talk, and you'll change your attitude. Before taking another step, let's summarize with the **Civility Wrap-up** and then be sure you **C's the Day**!

Civility Wrap-Up

- Don't buy into your negative self-talk.

- Be kind, generous, and honest with yourself. But be accountable!

- Take these 10 steps to protect yourself in a toxic workplace:

  - Focus First

  - Follow through from the Beginning

  - Interact with Others in Mind

  - Express Yourself

  - Be Your Own Choreographer

  - Pull Out the Mirror

  - Make an Entrance

  - Take Notes

  - Create a New Commentary

  - Change the Scenery

C's the Day

Please consider your own internal commentary and review my explanation of why all that negativity is inaccurate. Then, please consider all ten steps with specifics in mind. Whether it's selecting specific radio stations or music artists, write down how you will follow-through with each step. With everything spelled out on paper, begin the process of making each of these ten steps habit! It takes practice!

Communicating Character by Exercising Civility

NOTES CHAPTER 13

1 *Rolling Stone*, "Playlist: Michael Phelps' Solid-Gold Hits," www.rollingstone.com/music/news/playlist-michael-phelps-solid-gold-hits-20120816.

CONCLUSION
C's the Day...
Day after Day

I am confident that you now know what it means to unleash civility!

You now see civility in an entirely new light. You know that it is not some fragile behavior to be used only on special occasions like grandma's best china. Civility is a force that embodies strength, energy, and thought; its use requires daily practice. The respect that results from civility motivates and inspires honesty and frankness—two elements vital to success or failure. With civility, confrontation is valued, not feared. Civility demands politeness, and delivers trust. Civility doesn't make excuses, it consciously chooses to do the right thing—even when it's not the easy thing. When civility is unleashed, both you and your business can experience magnificent results.

You have challenged old definitions and impressions and replaced them with new, different, and empowering approaches to civility-based behavior. You've done the work to **C's the Day**—every day. Each exercise has moved you closer to making civility a living and breathing part of you. Every time you completed an exercise and put your findings into effect, you strengthened your civility muscle, improved your flexibility, and made your heart appreciative and more powerful.

Others may undervalue and underuse civility, but you now hold a secret that not only sets you apart, but makes a positive difference in the work you do and in the lives you touch. You now not only understand its influence, but you've begun to take the steps to integrate civility into your mindset and behavior in both your personal and professional life. If your organization just needs a shot of vitamin C—civility, that is— undoubtedly you realize that you can personally be the impetus that launches respect, courtesy, and thoughtfulness to a higher level.

Like any endeavor we undertake for self-improvement, civility makes its demands. It demands the best of you. Civility pushes you and pulls you and demands that you be more to yourself, to others, to your organization, and to your society. You are consistent and dedicated, and you are redefining yourself into your best self.

If you are now enmeshed in a toxic situation and find yourself overwhelmed, as I was that Christmas when I sat on my couch in tears, please know that the lessons in this book can help you. Not for a moment do I believe that your sprinkling of civility in an overwhelmingly toxic situation will transform the ugly to the lovely. The easy answer is to walk away; sadly for many, that is not an option. My wish is that you take the tools in this book and unleash civility within yourself as your personal shield to protect you from barbs, accusations, and rudeness. Strengthening yourself will not only help you to stand tall and breathe deeply, but will replace the negative views with more positive outlooks in your relationships with those you hold dear during this tumultuous time.

My goal in this book was for you to gain a newfound respect for civility and to learn what it can bring to you, your workplace, your professional relationships, and your financial success. I hope your renewed appreciation for civility is a catalyst that motivates you, your teams, and your organization toward behavior that is grounded in civility. I also hope that you now look at this enigmatic word with awe, wonder, and affection. I appreciate that you stuck in there with me! And at the very least, I trust your eyes no longer glaze over at the mere mention of civility.

Finally, please don't underestimate your effect on others—the people with whom you have direct contact and the people whom you touch in conversation. Remember the power of **The 3 C's: You *Communicate* your *Character* by how you exercise your *Civility*!**

ABOUT THE AUTHOR

Diana Damron is a former television anchor and reporter who uses her well-honed skills of communication to transform businesses, organizations, and individuals. Today Diana is a speaker and trainer, as well as a personal and executive coach. Diana spent years in front of the camera and behind the scenes to interview the famous, the infamous, and those who just have a story to tell. After experiencing both the positive and dark side of work environments, Diana used her skills to develop The 3 C's approach to detect what specifically is holding back a company or an individual from achieving success and personal satisfaction. Diana uses Civility, Communication, and Character (The 3 C's) to take organizations and individuals from toxic to trusting. Diana also prepares and coaches individuals—whether executive or at-home-entrepreneur—to speak before audiences whether in the board room or on stage. In person, in front of an audience, and in writing, Diana's work is laced with humor. After all, this is the woman who walked right off the runway and fell into the laps of the stunned crowd at a national modeling competition at the Waldorf Astoria in New York City. You can see Diana's TedxTalk on "The Force of Civility" through her website or through YouTube.com. For information on training, keynotes, fees, and availability, please visit Diana's website at **DianaDamron.com** or email her at **Diana@DianaDamron.com**.

33575702R00108

Made in the USA
Middletown, DE
18 July 2016